Contents

*"I will build a motor car for the great multitude.
It will be large enough for the family, but small enough for the
individual to run and care for. It will be constructed of the best
materials, by the best men to be hired, after the simplest designs
that modern engineering can devise. But it will be so low in price
that no man making a good salary will be unable to own—and
enjoy with his family the blessings of hours of pleasure in God's
great open spaces."*

Henry Ford, 1907

FORD
MODEL T
CATALOG OF ACCESSORIES

The F-B Oil Saver
for FORDS

Patent
Pending $

STOPS OIL PUMPING
STOPS SPARK PLUG FOU
SAVES 50% LUBRICATIN
SAVES TIME—SAVES M

Thousands are using them.
today for one on 30-day tria'
paid for $1.00. Money back
satisfied. No cost to instal
places breather cap on oil filli

Dealers Wanted

PENINSULAR CORPORATION, Penobscot Bldg., Dep
For $1.00 enclosed send me an F-B Oil S
money-back guarantee if not satisfactory.

Gordon Schindl

Publishers & Wh

First published in 1991 by Motorbooks International Publishers & Wholesalers, P.O. Box 2, 729 Prospect Avenue, Osceola, WI 54020 USA

Motorbooks International books are also available at discounts in bulk quantity for industrial or sales-promotional use. For details write to Special Sales Manager at the Publisher's address

Library of Congress Cataloging-in-Publication Data
Schindler, Gordon
    Ford Model T catalog of accessories / Gordon
    Schindler.
    p. cm.
    ISBN 0-87938-492-1
    1. Ford Model T automobile—Parts—Catalogs.
    I. Title.
TL215.F75S35   1991
629.28'722—dc20   90-48365

"My Experiences With the Model T" and "The Ubiquitous Model T" reprinted with permission of Intertech Publishing. Photo of L. L. Corum and his 1923 Model T racer courtesy of Indianapolis Motor Speedway. All other photos, from Mr. Schindler's personal collection.

Printed and bound in the United States of America

Buyer Beware

An introduction to the various fast-buck artists,
garage inventors, miracle carburetor salesmen
and the odd truly honest aftermarket
Model T parts supplier

The more successful a product is, the greater the chance of someone trying to improve on it.

As improbable as that may sound, it's true — especially in the automotive industry in the field of replacement or aftermarket parts. At least this was true up to the mid thirties when dozens, if not hundreds, of replacement and improvement parts were offered automobilists, primarily by mail-order firms.

All too often such improvement devices were the efforts of fast-buck artists, ready to take advantage of an obvious opportunity created by the myriad items which go into making an automobile. All these items were manufactured down to a price, even in the most successful of cars, resulting in products which were far from mechanical perfection.

These circumstances led to a compromise between quality and price, resulting in "the best car that could

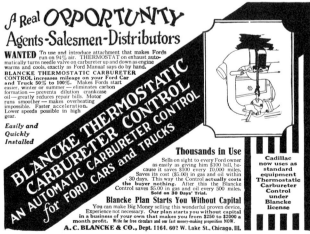

Ad for Blancke Thermostatic Carburetor Control notes that it is now used as standard equipment on Cadillacs — it must be good for a Ford!

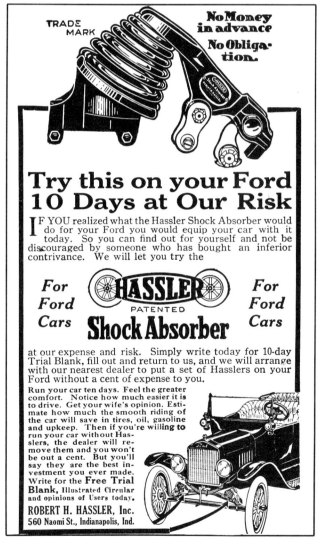

An ad for the Hassler Shock Absorber.

be produced for the money." The lower the production cost, the greater the possibility of someone ultimately offering a product that either was omitted from the car or improved upon an existing feature. Just as there was a maximum manufacturing cost set for the complete car, so there was a maximum price for individual parts. A small saving on a single part could add up to a considerable sum, when production ultimately amounted to millions of units.

The question of whether a new product is as good as or superior to the product it is replacing is a valid one, especially in the automotive parts replacement industry. Making such a determination has been difficult in the past, due to a lack of adequate impartial testing concerns. All one had to go on were the claims of the part manufacturer—needless to say, usually not a reliable guide.

The ads in this book have been selected as sound representations of products worth serious considera-

tion by any Model T or Model A owner of the period—with, perhaps, a few questionable examples. Two obvious facts emerge from even a cursory examination of these ads: first, almost all of these products were offered by manufacturers, most of whom have disappeared, who sprang up to promote a specific original product; and second, the overwhelming number of these products have failed to stand the test of time.

Most of these firms were not put out of business because their products were adopted by auto manufacturers. However, they would have been happy to have sold to them, and there is more than one instance in which this seems to have been the case. In one ad from 1925, it is stated that "Cadillac now uses as standard equipment Thermostatic Carburetor Control under Blancke license."

Many of these aftermarket devices no doubt worked—at least to some degree. Even the successful

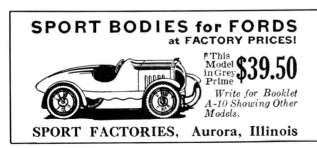

The Hassler Shock Absorber seen on a Ford Model T at a 1980s old car get-together in Los Angeles—still absorbing shocks!

An ad for Ford Sports Bodies at a mere $39.50.

A 1908 Ford ad for the four cylinder Touring car. This was the first Model T advertisement.

THE COUPE
$520

Easier to handle—safer to drive

The driving control of the Ford car is exceedingly simple, yet always dependable. It effectively reduces the possibilities of accidents—particularly in crowded city traffic. Foot pedal gear changing, powerful brakes, short wheelbase and full visibility, afforded by the all-steel body construction with narrower pillars and large plate-glass windows, are important reasons why Ford owners enjoy such security. Let the nearest Authorized Ford Dealer explain the many features of Ford cars and demonstrate their easy handling. Get full particulars about convenient time payment plans.

RUNABOUT, $260 • TOURING, $290 • COUPE, $520
TUDOR SEDAN, $580 • FORDOR SEDAN, $660
Closed cars in colors. • Demountable rims and starter
extra on open cars.   *All prices F. O. B. Detroit*

FORD MOTOR COMPANY, DETROIT, MICH.

BEAUTY ·, COMFORT ·, CONVENIENCE ·, UTILITY

The 1925 Ford Model T Coupe. This was one of the last Model T advertisements.

ones failed eventually, however; as production vehicles steadily improved, rendering these independent products ineffective. The classical example is the device which promised greater fuel economy by merely increasing the amount of air in the fuel mixture. Modern antipollution equipment now has thinned out the fuel mixture to such an extent that these devices can't be used effectively. A return to less stringent regulations still would not enable these devices to return to life: such a change is not likely to happen, as indicated by an article in today's newspaper which reported the introduction of new and more sweeping clean air bills in Congress.

Those who have impartially examined the products in question have reported almost unani-

Everything for the Ford owner—and only twenty-five cents!

Slip seat covers for comfort and durability on 1913–1915 Model Ts.

mously of their ineffectiveness, which brings to mind the old saying, "If it sounds too good to be true, it probably is." Even at this date, no carburetor has been found which comes anywhere near doubling gas mileage. No spark plug booster or intensifier has appeared which will boost either mileage or performance. The same can be said of spark plugs, with all the claims of superior performance. The plug makers are still grinding out much the same plugs they made fifty years ago.

It should be pointed out, in all fairness, that the Model T, or even the Model A, was not made to compete with the Packard or Pierce Arrow. During the early days of the automobile industry, manufacturing techniques were limited. Compounding these limitations was the ever-growing demand for automobiles. The successful companies at least could sell all the cars they could produce. Why waste time or money trying to improve on success? People like Harold Wills are reputed to have stopped production lines to incorporate improvements in their product, delaying deliveries to what customers they did have. Today, who remembers the Wills-St. Claire?

The trend today, aside from performance items, is in the field of replacement parts for the Model T and the Model A. These are either NOS (new old stock) or newly-manufactured parts. Publications devoted to this field, such as *Old Cars Weekly, Hemmings Motor News* and *Cars & Parts*, contain many ads of firms offering both NOS and newly-made parts—guaranteed to be identical to the original!

A J. C. Whitney catalog of a few years ago contained several pages of newly-manufactured old parts. Stated to be manufactured to original specifications were such items as exhaust systems, headlight lenses, transmission linings and bushings, ring and pinion gear sets, ignition parts, rear axles, timers, coils and points. The catalog even contained sheet metal parts such as hoods and trunk compartments, not to mention rumble seats, splash pans and floor paneling. All these parts were guaranteed to be duplicates of the originals—"perfect for authentic restoration, repairing, or replacing rusted or missing panels. Construction of heavy gauge steel—holes drilled for easy installation." So went Whitney's guarantee.

Also available were "Fiberglass Parts for 1923 T Roadster. Authentic "23 'T-Bucket' body [which] is an exact reproduction of the original."

The ultimate in reproduction of old parts was, of course, the reproduction of complete 1930 Model As, and, recently, even 1932 Model Bs.

Gordon Schindler
Redondo Beach, CA
August 1990

Chapter 1

The Ubiquitous Model T

Les Henry

The Model T combined the web-footedness of the duck with the agility of the mountain goat

So much has already been written and so much is still remembered from firsthand experience concerning the Model T Ford that there seems little of value left upon which to expound; but, with no pretense to be either encyclopedic or yet entirely original, this writing is humbly dedicated to those of us now interested in Model T Fords who never before knew them, or, having known, forgot.

While mundane, the Model T was never mediocre. In its day it commanded honest respect for the service it rendered and for the revolution it wrought, and in our day, it commands a place of honor in our museums and private collections of venerable motor cars. Uncompromisingly erect, unquestionably ugly, funereally drab, the Model T combined the web-footedness of the duck with the agility of the mountain goat; it could go anywhere—except in society. And though seemingly conceived in madness, there is something immortal about this strange little car.

Lee Strout White thought to mark its passing in 1936 with his humorous and knowing article, "Farewell My Lovely," and he marveled then that Sears & Roebuck's catalog listed parts for 1909–27 Fords. Well, it still does! Statistically, the T is with us yet, for as late as 1949, there were more than 200,000 registered in the United States, more than all the automobiles registered in the country when the Model T was created, just forty years before.

From October 1908 until May 1927, there flowed an almost unbroken flood of Model Ts, all from the same mold but still not identical to the final total of over fifteen million. No other automobile model even began to approach such volume and only Rolls-Royce with their Silver Ghost (1907–27) enjoyed such a [long] production record. During most of this time, Ford produced as many or more than all other Ameri-

can car manufacturers combined, and during all this time, the Model T, often modified, was never basically changed. It is these myriad and often subtle modifications which interest many of us today. It is these that spark many a debate and bring strong men to their knees before the Model T to prove a point in question. Let us look into the seeming paradox of change in the changeless Model T.

While it is not usually difficult for those knowledgeable to establish the age of a Model T by certain features peculiar to a certain particular 'style year,' no generalization concerning the Model T is ever safe. Too many minute changes were constantly being worked upon it for the purposes of speeding production, cutting costs, or, to a very limited degree, increasing customer appeal. Many arguments are engendered today by such simple facts as the appearance of plain hoods on some Ts in 1915 (which 'style year'

Model T parts available everywhere, cheap!

featured the first louvered hoods) and the appearance of both plain and lipped front fenders on the pre-1917 models.

Actually, Model T cars continued during a given production year did vary in many points and were never so much alike as 'peas in a pod' as legend would have us believe. Variations also resulted from the necessity of having parts made by several different contractors. It was not until the 1920s that Ford finally attained his goal of producing one hundred percent of the car in his own factories.

Typical of Ford's cost-cutting program was the fate of the full-leather upholstering prevalent through 1912. This gave way to leatherette door panels in 1913 and was followed by leatherette back cushions in 1914, all of which yielded to full-leatherette patches only on the the doors in 1915-16. Even this vestige of leatherette was replaced in late 1916 by cheap, pressed steel caps at the doors. While these are indeed generalizations, they serve to illustrate the many constant changes in the interest of cost-reduction during that period when Ford had the whole industry in a dizzy spin. This was the time that Ford introduced the $5 day, the $500 car and the $50 refund to customers.

Cost-cutting did not result in any loss of quality in the Model T, except in the sense that luxury appointments not affecting serviceability were lost. Simple in the extreme and lacking in many comforts, the Model T seemed always to run despite its adversity. Into the vital parts went vanadium alloys, new to the automotive industry in 1908. While the structural, mechanical and economic advantages of *en bloc* cylinder casting had been seen by others before, Ford extended this idea to include the upper crankcase with main bearings as an *en bloc* casting, with a removable cylinder head.

Although the principle of mass production had been practiced for half a century by arms manufacturers, Ford applied it to the automotive industry in a successful and spectacular way. And then, years ahead of the times, Ford seemed to sit back and watch, as the Model T clattered over the entire nation, the continent and finally, the world.

Doubtless the greatest controversy among Ford devotees centers around the alleged '1908' Model T. Let there be no doubt on this point. There never was a 1908 Model T! The Ford car for 1908 was the Model S. For 1909 it was the Model T, born in the new Piquette Avenue factory in Detroit in October 1908. True, there were actually 308 Model T cars built during the last quarter of 1908 but these were acclaimed the new 1909 style and were always referred to as such in contemporary Ford literature and parts catalogs. For the purpose of dating any automobile, we can accept only the model or 'style year,' rather than the actual date of manufacture of an individual car. This is in line with the long-established practice by nearly all established automobile makers, including Ford, to introduce a new style at some time other than on New Year's Day.

It would be much less confusing for us today if the Model T actually had been presented as the 1908 style, for those produced after April differed so vastly from the earlier 1909 Fords as to constitute an evident, though not acclaimed, style change. Ford always referred to these as "the 1909 Fords under number 2,500." We cannot now do otherwise. Rarest of the 1909 Fords were, and still are, those of the first 1,000 which were characterized by having the wheel brake and reverse band operated by individual and distinctly different hand levers. Ford quickly abandoned this method late in February, in favor of the well-known three-pedal system and encouraged the conversion of all previously-produced Ts to the three-pedal system by offering owners new parts at a cost of $15, but requiring the return of all original parts to the factory.

Easy starting, easy running—most of the time.

Handles easily in all emergencies.

So thoroughly was the hand lever reverse system thus eradicated that in later years, Ford, wishing to restore a very early Model T to his museum, had to *reinstall* a reverse lever, unfortunately, however, using for the purpose a brake lever and failing to remove the ratchet release handle! Publicity, being what it is, this car is erroneously claimed to be a '1908' Model T Ford. It would indeed be interesting to know just how many Model T cars numbered under 1,000 are in existence today, and of these, how many still have the two-lever system intact.

The first 2,500 Model T Fords were equipped with a centrifugal water pump, had slightly shorter engine blocks and crankshafts, and had very small commutators, commonly called 'timers' today. These and other such features meant that the latter-day Ts had parts that were not interchangeable with earlier parts. Thus, today a collector fortunate enough to find an early Model T will be unfortunate in a search for parts.

As the demand for gasoline increased, particularly during World War I, its quality was decreased in favor of volume until the late twenties. This held back automobile engine performance. Under these conditions, while the Model T progressed in style, size, appointments and weight, it retrogressed in engine performance. The early Model T engines had the highest compression, 60 pounds per square inch (psi), with approximately a 4.5:1 compression ratio. This permitted the development of 22 hp. These characteristics were first introduced in 1912, again for 1915, and finally, were set in 1917 with compression at 45 psi and a 3.98:1 ratio. This resulted in 20 hp. Maximum horsepower was developed at 1500 rpm and produced a road

Stops instantly—upon application of brake, clutch and reverse pedals.

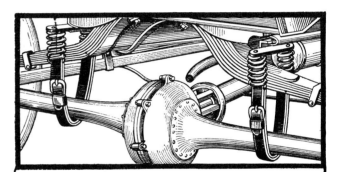

A 1922 ad for a shock absorber to improve the springing on the Model T. Shocks were adopted later but not this primitive type.

No special gasoline necessary. High octane may even be dangerous!

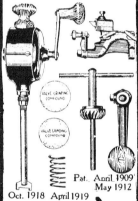
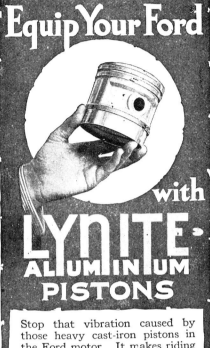

speed of 37 miles per hour, at which point the 'pulling power' or torque had dropped to 70 lb-ft.

With a few notable exceptions, the bodies were of wood until the 1911 style was advanced with sheet metal applied over a wooden frame. Some few touring cars in 1909 had sheet aluminum bodies. It is interesting to note that the 1913 style was the first Ford touring car to have front doors designed into the body and that the left front door was a dummy and remained as such (except in the Canadian Fords) until 1926. In 1912, a 'Fore-Door' version of the touring car appeared with factory-fitted front door units. These were actually removable and could be purchased as parts for adding to the 1911–12 touring cars already in use.

All radiators of the Model T 'brass era' ending September 1916 were dimensionally the same but differed in that the first 2,500 had a leading and trailing stroke (often called wings) on the Ford script pressed into the radiator tank, while some very few of these bore no name at all. The later brass radiators displayed the Ford script in its familiar form.

The winged script and the block lettered Ford hubcaps were but carryover details of the previous 1908 Model S. The V-shaped radiators sometimes seen were not genuine Ford products, simply a dress-up item, as were wooden top trim on the doors, coil-spring shock absorbers, demountable rims, electric conversion units for gas lamps, lined wheel-brake shoes, thirty-minute transmission bands, and mechanical starters. Whole industries sprang up and prospered in supplying gadgets to overcome real and imaginary deficiencies of the Model T. Some of these items were actually improvements and later adopted by the factory.

In this vein, it is interesting to note that a Hind-View Auto Reflector was offered as a new accessory made expressly for Fords by Kales-Haskel in August 1911 — interesting because this was only three months after the 1911 Indianapolis Race wherein Ray Harroun innovated the rearview mirror on his winning Marmon Wasp.

The 1914 style Model T, while similar to the 1913, except for door shape, was the last seen exhibiting the truly antique appearance afforded by the straight line fenders, front and rear, the acetylene gas lamps and the bulb horn.

Then came the transitional form of Model T which, while holding somewhat to the old, reached out toward the new. Two enclosed body types were presented for 1915 in the preceding November: the Sedan with two central side doors and the Coupelet, the first convertible coupe. The open-body types were continued unchanged until April 1915, and must even now be considered as 1914 type Ts, although built in 1915. The new-style cars were characterized principally by the magneto-powered electric headlamps, the straight front but curved rear fenders, the louvers in the little boxlike engine hood, the hand Claxon and

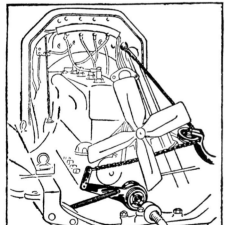
An ad for a mechanical-type starter for the Model T, circa 1918.

the recessed steel cowl fairing, sharply out to the body and mounting an unbraced windshield. No significant changes appeared in 1916, except for the elimination of brass from lamp rims and tops. For taillights, the little round-bodied, black oil lamps remained standard for yet a decade on the lowest-priced types of Ts, side lamps having been eliminated in 1921.

But a completely new look came to the Model T with the 1917 style. Front and rear fenders both were curved and crowned, the engine hood was enlarged, fairly smoothly from the higher, smarter (and cheaper!) pressed-steel radiator shell, right up to the sharply curved cowl. This comparatively tremendous advance in styling served to set a pattern for most of the succeeding decade.

Unchanged in size or appearance, the Model T gained mechanical improvements in 1919, in the form of an electric starter and demountable rims as limited optional equipment.

The year 1923 brought refinements of lines and trim, featuring lowered bodies and the introduction of the one-man top and the four-door sedan.

Like Ford himself, the Model T was a paradox. Ford continually resisted change — yet changed. He professed scorn of history, yet spent millions to perpetuate the Edison Institute. To demands for a change in the Model T, Ford always replied "Why change, when we can't make enough as it is?" Even in 1924–25, when the Model T floated out of Dearborn on balloon

tires, some models were still offered sans starter and defiantly wearing the little oil taillamp as a badge of Ford's resistance to change!

It has often been stated that Ford maintained two production lines, one for cars and one for jokes, but this is apocryphal. However, both were legion and Ford, quick to appreciate the free advertising value of such jokes, actually promulgated them. He was more interested in their effect than their veracity, of course. Witness his own jest apropos color for the Model T, "The customer may have any color he wants — as long as it is black!" This the public heard and remembered, forgetting the colorful Model Ts of 1909-13, and shrugged off those of 1926-27.

Then, in a final splash of color, and after a heroic essay on glamour, the Model T was finally stricken from the production schedule in June 1927. For a while, parts were stockpiled. Then the 1908 models were discarded as Ford enthusiastically produced the equally famous Model A.

But the inertia of fifteen million Model T Fords is not yet spent!

Toward the goal of more positive identifications and to aid in more authentic restorations of these antique Fords, this resume of progressive changes in the Model T is hopefully directed. Some information which might have been included here was not for want of its complete verification or because of its availability in Ford handbooks.

An early mail-order catalog ad, offering what appears to be genuine replacement carburetor for the Model T.

Model T Tips and Suggestions

Towing

Never tow a Model T Ford except in an emergency because of the unit power-plant design which depends on the rapid rotation of the engine flywheel for lubrication of all parts, including clutch and throw-out bearing. Towing the Model T in neutral results in damage to clutch parts and transmission bands for want of lubrication.

If the car must be towed, then do so with the clutch engaged in high-speed position and with spark plugs removed so the engine may turn over freely. Keep towing speed below 25 miles per hour. In dire cases where a tow truck must be engaged, lift the rear wheels, lock the steering, and tow the Model T backwards on the front wheels.

An alternative method, requiring considerable effort, is to remove the universal joint before towing.

Storing

When storing a Model T, even if only overnight, the high-speed clutch should be engaged. This forces the hot oil between the plates of the multiple-disk clutch, thereby reducing transmission drag on the engine when cranking for starting (in neutral, of course) later. This is particularly true in cold weather.

Starting

Always unpredictable, the Model T sometimes fails to respond to the usual methods of starting, even when interspersed with the usually effective invectives, maledictions, imprecations and profanations. In such cases, when even the de-oiled clutch fails to help, there is yet a way to coax life into the old Model T. Jack up one rear wheel, chock the others fore and aft, engage the high-speed clutch, set the spark and gas, then spin the crank. This bypasses the metaphysical transmission and allows the rear wheel to act as a flywheel connected directly to the engine. This method rarely fails.

Sometimes it does, though. Then, if there is any glimmer of spark at all, a shot of ether (sulfuric, not petroleum) from a medicine dropper into the intake manifold or the carburetor of the Model T will bring forth a tumultuous roar of explosions from the engine. After a little of this, even the most recalcitrant of Model T Fords will catch on and run without further hypodermics.

Never race a cold Model T engine; the pistons will break!

Overheating

The "antique" Fords will tend to overheat if driven too fast for any distance because the little brass radiators were somewhat undersized. The Model T can actually run so hot that shutting off the ignition will not stop the engine. It continues to run after the fashion of a diesel! This is disastrous because if the bearings do not burn out, the magneto magnets will surely become demagnetized and an engine overhaul will be necessary.

Lubrication

Straight mineral oils (without additives) of SAE 10 for winter and SAE 20 grade for summer in well-adjusted engines are recommended, if this oil is drained and changed frequently. Because of the somewhat limited usage given most antique cars, the heavy-duty or detergent oils will prove valuable in preventing sludging, valve and ring sticking, and rusting of internal surfaces

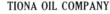

A 1918 ad for Ford Special oil.

Above copy was placed on windshields of early Model Ts.

As a supplement to manuals which tell the how of the Model T, this summary attempts to tell the what and the when. Listed only are new items and changes peculiar to each production year and, where no further reference is made, such items may be considered as continued unchanged during the ensuing years. Typical of the antique stylings are Model T Ford specifications published January 1912.

1909 Ford Model T

The newly designed Ford, Model T, was introduced in October 1908.

Types and prices

Touring	Runabout	Coupe	Town	Tourster
$850	$825	$950	$1,000	NA

Salient features: 'Winged' Ford name on radiator tank; one-piece oilpan; flat, rectangular door on transmission cover; open valve chambers.

Engine

Engines under number 1,000 (late February) had a low, flat cylinder head drilled for fifteen ⅜ in. cap bolts. Compression was 60 psi; and ratio was about 4.5: 1. No name appeared on head or on transmission cover door.

Engines under number 2,500 (mid-April) had a slightly higher cylinder head for greater water capacity; the head remained flat but was drilled for fifteen 7/16 in. cap bolts and bore the name Ford Motor Co. in block letters. All these engines were further characterized by the absence of a front water jacket and by the inclusion of a water pump, a gear driven from the camshaft and carrying an eight-bladed fan on the end of the pump shaft. A long oil-fill tube (pipe) was attached on top of crankcase at left front; the engine number appeared on a boss near the bottom of front cylinder at the right. The crankshaft was only 25 in. long; the heavy connecting rods were bronze-bushed for a wrist pin held tight in the piston.

The Ford name appeared in script on transmission cover door.

Engines above the number 2,500 had no water pumps but were cooled by thermosyphon effect. Therefore the cylinder head was again given greater water capacity with a jacket dome sloping forward to a vertical hose connection. The block was altered because of elimination of the water pump and the water jacket was extended around the front. The crankshaft length was increased to 25 5/32 in. and fitted with a pulley for a flat belt drive to the four-bladed fan. The timing cover was altered and included an integrally cast oil-fill spout.

The commuter was changed (enlarged) and this remained as standard equipment thereafter. Connecting rods were lightened slightly, and the bushing was omitted; shaft end was bored to 1½ in. with ⅛ in. of babbitt thickness. Cylinder bore and stroke remained at 3¾ x 4 in. with a displacement of 176.7 cubic inches.

Bodies

Colors were optional; black, red, green, blue, pearl gray or French gray were available. Wood was the standard material for construction but a few Touring Cars had sheet aluminum bodies, presumably experimental. For this year only, the Tourster body was offered having no doors at all and having identical front and rear seat assemblies. The Coupe was distinguished by having the doors hinged at the rear.

Running boards were of wood, covered with linoleum on cars under number 2,500 but were later of pressed steel with several rows of interrupted ridges running lengthwise. No Ford script appeared on any of these. Fenders were steel, flat-topped and rimmed, and were generally square-ended, though often lipped in front. Fender finish was always in black japan. Engine hoods were 24 in. long for Runabouts, 22 in. long for all other types until 1917.

Steering gear

This 50 in. assembly was fitted for a wooden wheel of 13 in. outside diameter, had a brass spider and had a brass case for the planetary steering gears mounted directly under the spider. Steering ratio was three-to-one reduction.

Running gear

Standard tread was 56 in., with 60 in. optional for the Southern trade, where wagon ruts were wider. Peculiar to the early Fords was the pressed-steel, riveted differential and axle housing which contained straight (untapered) axles and driveshaft running in bronze bushings; only the outer axle bearings were roller.

Ignition

Alternating current was generated by sixteen V-shaped magnets 9/16 in. wide clamped to the flywheel and rotated past a ring of sixteen coils fixed to the in-side of the transmission case; voltages up to 28 were obtained, varying with engine speed. This low-tension current was distributed by the commutator, or timer, to four vibrator spark coils contained in a wooden case on the dashboard, thence as high-tension current to the spark plugs. These were eight Heinze coils or were Kingston coils.

Lamps and accessories

The all-brass lamps included two 8 in. acetylene gas head lamps, with a brass generator, two square oil sidelamps, and a square taillamp. The bulb horn and all other accessories were of polished brass.

1910 Ford Model T

Essentially identical to the last 1909 Fords, the 1910 style was announced in October 1909.

Types and prices (August)

Touring	Runabout	Coupe	Town	Torpedo
$950	$900	$1,050	$1,200	NA

A 1910 Ford ad, replete with Ford's financial confidence.

A 1910 Ford ad: "Ford does not want sales that are made only because of price."

Salient features: Ford name appeared in script along with the diamond designs pressed into running boards.

Engine

Changes were not obvious, consisting principally of an alteration in the method of fastening magnets to the flywheel starting in March (engine number 17500) and a second alteration of the flywheel itself to accommodate the larger ⅝ in. magnets installed in May (engine number 20500) to increase magneto power.

The standard carburetor was the Kingston Model L-2.

Bodies

No changes were offered except for the new Torpedo Roadster, a racy looking car which featured low doors, a curved front and rear fenders, a 16 gallon fuel tank and a toolbox mounted on rear deck. The long, 61 in. steering column and the windshield were set at a rakish angle to carry out the suggestion of speed. And, with its high-compression engine, light flywheel (including magneto) and light, low body, this car had undoubtedly the best performance and greatest speed of any Model T produced. At this time, the doors on the Coupe were hinged in front.

On New Year's Eve, cars were shipped from the Piquette Avenue, Detroit, plant for the last time. On the first day of 1910 deliveries were made from the new Highland Park plant.

1911 Ford Model T

Many engineering advances appeared in the 1911 style Fords, brought out in October 1910.

Types and prices (August)

Touring	Runabout	Coupe	Town	Torpedo
$750	$680	$1,050	$1,200	NA

Salient features: Removable connecting rod pan; larger steering wheel; larger transmission cover door; metal bodies.

Engine

Most welcome was the inclusion of a removable connecting rod pan, obviating the necessity of removing the entire engine and all forward body parts to adjust rod bearings. With this change came a larger, sloping access door for easier adjustment of the transmission bands, and the clutch pedal was altered to fit this enlarged transmission cover. The engine number

The 1911 five-passenger Touring Car, complete with bulb horn and gas headlights.

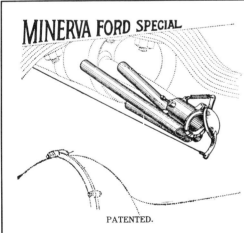
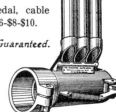
The Minerva Horns with their "celebrated musical voice" were operated off of the Model T's exhaust gases.

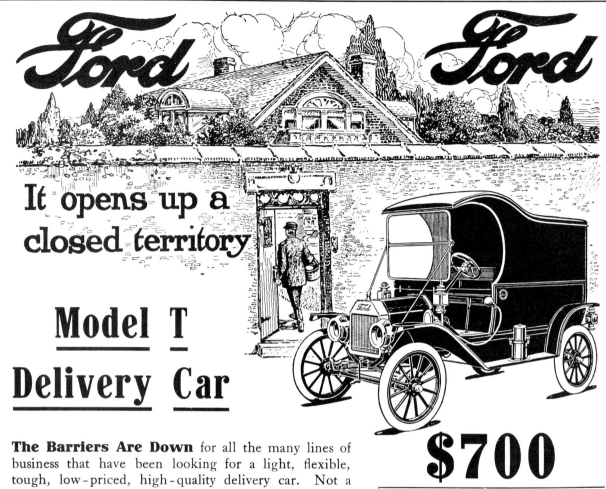

It opens up a closed territory

Model T Delivery Car

$700

This price includes full equipment—Automatic Brass Windshield, Speedometer, Ford Magneto built into the motor, two six-inch Gas Lamps and Generator, three Oil Lamps, Horn and Tools. No Ford cars sold unequipped.
Capacity, 750 pounds of Merchandise.

The Barriers Are Down for all the many lines of business that have been looking for a light, flexible, tough, low-priced, high-quality delivery car. Not a truck nor a van, but a CAR—that can cover the ground, open up new territory, bring in new customers, advertise its owner, extend the business, outwork a team of horses and cut the maintenance bill. **That car is this FORD Model T Delivery.**

THERE IS NO CLOSED TERRITORY to the wholesaler, the retailer, the power or light company that uses the Ford Model T Delivery Car. It eats up space and annihilates time. It makes relics of more than a million old style delivery vehicles in the United States. It is the feature of 1912 in commercial automobiles. It advertises its dealers and booms its buyers.

TWO YEARS OF HARD PRACTICAL TEST lie behind this statement of fact. The Wanamaker stores of New York and Philadelphia, and the Bell Telephone Company all over the Country, have taken these Ford Model T Delivery Cars and driven them now for over two years, winter and summer, uphill and down. No factory test here, but the actual grind of work. Result—not a change. The guarantee of Accomplishment stands on this car.

Light: weighs 1200 pounds—low tire expense—less fuel, multiplies the actual horsepower—carries 750 pounds of merchandise—carries it anywhere, any time.

Flexible: turns in a circle of 28 feet—accommodates itself to owner's and customers' space.

Tough: the same strong chassis of all Ford Model T cars—same simplicity of operation, same Ford magneto built into the motor, same Vanadium steel throughout (40 locomotives of vanadium at twice the cost of carbon steel are now being considered by the Secretary of War for use at Panama).

Low-priced: completely equipped—$700—no more than a team and wagon.

High-quality: stands side by side with the other productions of Ford genius—with more than 100,000 drivers vouching for them.

Your competition is active. Think hardest and FIRST. Send for our descriptive booklet. Ford branches and dealers everywhere.

Good dealers in unoccupied territory are requested to write us.

Ford Motor Company

Detroit, Michigan, U. S. A.

A 1911 Ford ad for a Model T Delivery Car: "It opens up a closed territory."

was relocated to the boss over the water hose connection on left of the block.

Enclosure of the valve chambers, entailing a second alteration of the engine block casting, was introduced later on in the year. Along with this came steel valve push rods replacing the former brass ones.

Bodies

During this year, sheet metal bodies became standard but resembled the former wooden ones closely.

Steering gear

This assembly was lengthened to 56 in. and the steering wheel diameter increased to 15 in.

Running gear

The driveshaft and the axles were each tapered at one end and were carried entirely on roller bearings instead of partly in bushings; a malleable-iron spool piece was inserted between the shaft housing and the differential housing to contain the new roller and ball thrust driveshaft bearings.

The front-wheel steering knuckle and spindle unit was assembled of two pieces to simplify forging and remained unchanged until 1917. A larger ball and socket was fitted in the front radius-rod unit.

Lamps

Magneto-powered electric conversion units were offered for the first time by K-W Company for Ford gas headlamps. Ford warned that the magneto was not powerful enough for lights and ignition, too. Sidelamp brackets were changed from round brass to flat iron.

1912 Ford Model T

October 1911 saw the first of the new 1912 style Fords.

Types and prices

Touring	Runabout	Town	Torpedo	Fore-Door
$690	$590	$900	NA	NA

Engine

For the first time, the engine compression ratio was slightly lowered by enlarging combustion space in the cylinder head.

A third change in timing-gear cover plate introduced the usual timer with a built-in oil-fill spout. This was soon abandoned in favor of the fourth-type cover plate, more like the earlier type, but having an adjustable screw for fan belt tension just above the integrally cast oil-fill spout, which itself was pierced by a cap screw.

Bodies

New in styling was the Fore-Door Touring Car, unique in that front, or fore, door units, were factory equipped. These units were subsequently made available as Ford accessories for shop installation in the regular 1911 or 1912 Touring Cars already in use.

A Torpedo Runabout was officially offered and for the last time this year, but it had not the rakish appearance nor yet the performance of the previous 1910–11 Torpedo. It was really the regular Runabout except for the curved fenders and 16 gallon round fuel tank mounted on the rear deck. The commercial Runabout was yet another modification, possessing a flat rear

A 1912 Model T station wagon. Such bodies were made by outside firms, with Ford supplying only the chassis and engine.

The business end of the station wagon. Note bulb horn and acetylene gas generator on running board.

deck for light freight with a single, detachable bucket seat on the toolbox, for the mother-in-law.

After 1912, the erect brass-bound, and brass-braced windshield were seen no more on new Fords; neither were the all-brass horn and lamps, nor the all-leather upholstery. Ford had begun to economize and to produce!

Steering gear

This was the last production year to have a cast-brass steering-wheel spider, though the brass steering-gear case remained until 1917.

1913 Ford Model T
Types and prices

Touring	Runabout	Town	Torpedo	Fore-Door
$690	$590	$900	NA	NA

Engine

The exhaust manifold and camshaft alterations were the only changes in the engine.

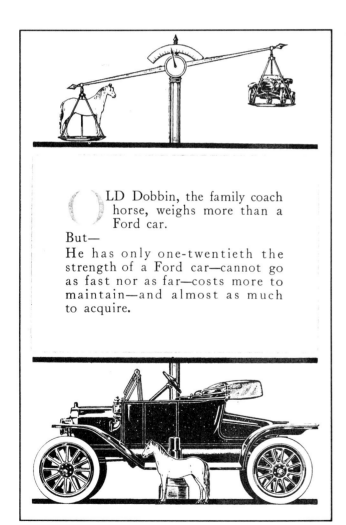

OLD Dobbin, the family coach horse, weighs more than a Ford car.

But—

He has only one-twentieth the strength of a Ford car—cannot go as fast nor as far—costs more to maintain—and almost as much to acquire.

A 1913 ad from Ford Times *comparing the weight and power of poor old Dobbin to the flivver. Naturally, the flivver won.*

Bodies

Last to be offered in colors and with factory striping, these were the first to have front doors designed into smooth-sided bodies; the tonneau was no longer a distinct division. A handle projected through the top edge of each door which was sharply rectangular in shape and which extended below the floor level to the top of the splash apron. Except for Fords produced in Canada and which are not considered in the scope of this treatise, the left front door was a dummy, access there being obstructed by the brake, anyway.

The cherry dashboard was continued, though reduced in size, to better fit the new body style. At this time, the windshield frame was changed from brass to steel, was mounted with the bottom section sloping backward, and was braced with short steel tubes to the top edge of the cowl. Ford script on the running board was changed from a longitudinal to a crosswise pattern.

Leatherette was employed for door panels only, while the upholstering remained in leather.

Steering gear

Cast steel replaced the brass steering spider, but the wooden wheel remained 15 in. in diameter.

Ignition

Far outnumbering the wooden coil boxes this year were the new, angular, pressed-steel coil boxes bearing the Ford name and containing K-W spark coils.

Lamps and accessories

Here, too, brass was largely replaced by steel, and black-painted lamps were furnished. The gas generator was made of iron instead of brass. The bulb horn, while still made of brass, was painted black, except for the belled end, and was mounted to project through the dashboard. A Stewart speedometer, chain-driven in a flexible housing from the right front wheel, was included at no extra cost. This, too, was black with a brass bezel.

1914 Ford Model T

Ford greeted the new year, January 1914, with a new style Model T.

Types and prices (August)

Touring	Runabout	Coupe	Town
$490	$440	$750	$690

Salient features: Black was the only color offered. Doors had rounded corners. Back cushions were leatherette and only the seats were leather. Profits were $30,000,000 for the fiscal year ending August.

Prices were actually lower than posted for all Fords sold between August 1914 and August 1915, at which time Ford announced a flat $50 refund for each customer in line with his profit-sharing plan. Yet the 1914 profits soared to $30,000,000 despite Ford's introduction of the $5 minimum payment for an eight-hour day. Competitors were paying an average of $2.34 for a nine-hour day!

Engine

The intake manifold was cast of iron instead of aluminum. Transmission cover door was of plain sheet steel stamping and no name appeared thereon. For the last time, pedals were initialed, and the crank was fitted with a curved aluminum handle.

Bodies

This was the last year in which Ford held to the truly "antique" styling. The bodies resembled those of 1913, having the small cherrywood dashboards and the straight, flat fenders. However, each door was rounded on the bottom corners which did not extend below the floor line. The latch handle extended through the inside panel rather than through the top of the door.

For the first time, front fenders were stamped with a strengthening rib across the widest portion. Up to and including 1914, windshields were similar in design though different in materials and mounting.

Running gear

The rear cross-member of the rectangular frame was lengthened, thereby eliminating the riveted attachment of brackets formerly used. Wheels were available in black or dark blue until 1920.

Ignition

Ford spark coils were introduced and the K-W and Heinze coils were altered to conform to the new standard size. All coils were housed in a pressed-steel box.

Lamps and accessories

Acetylene gas headlamps and square oil lamps were furnished for the last time with this style. All lamps and accessories were the same as offered in 1913, except for some lamp model changes.

1915 Ford Model T

The transitional styling of the Model T for 1915 appeared first in November 1914 with the closed cars, then in April 1915 for all types. Car number 1,000,000 was completed December 10.

Types and prices (August)

Touring	Runabout	Town	Sedan	Coupelet
$440	$390	$640	$750	$590

Salient features: Electric headlamps; louvered hood; curved rear fenders; metal cowl; round oil lamps.

Engine

Compression ratio was again lowered slightly. To supply the extra power required for lighting headlamps, the magneto coils were enlarged and the magnets were again increased in size to ¾ in. The transmission pedals were no longer initialed but had vertical ribs on the surface.

A medium-weight connecting rod was introduced, having a bore of 1⅜ in. and a babbitt thickness of ¹⁄₁₆ in.

Bodies

Starting November 1915, the new styling was offered only in two entirely new body types: the Sedan, having two central side doors, and the Coupelet, having the first convertible top. The Coupe was discontinued. Gone was the cherrywood dashboard, supplanted by a metal cowl sharply faired down to the original style, a boxlike engine hood which was still made of aluminum and was inletted with louvers. Until April 1915, the Touring, Runabout and Town types remained in the styling of 1914 and must be considered as such. Rear fenders were curved for the first time on all body types; front fenders remained straight, flat and, without exception, lipped. The windshield again became erect and was mounted without braces atop the cowl, immediately ahead of the doors.

Upholstering was entirely in leatherette on the open cars, except for a patch of leather at each door

A 1915 ad for refitting older Model Ts with genuine battery electric equipment, about the time the Model T adopted the same.

where the potential for wear was the greatest. The closed cars were upholstered in cloth.

Ignition

For the first time, all spark-coil boxes were made exactly alike of pressed steel with smooth corners and sloping top.

Lamps and accessories

Since the gas lamps were retained on some Fords until April, all cars until then had the forked lamp brackets even when fitted with electric lamps. But, when all types were at last equipped with the new 8½ in. electric headlamps, these were then mounted each on a single, flanged post. The light bulbs were of 9 volt capacity and were wired in series because the magneto voltage ranged from 8 to 28 volts or higher, depending on the engine speed. This arrangement was never entirely satisfactory, for at low speeds the lights were dim and, occasionally, at high speeds were so bright they could burn out.

Sidelamps were no longer different as to right or left, but were interchangeable, being rounded and symmetrical. The taillamp was similar to the sidelamps except for the ruby lens and a white side lens. All lamps were trimmed in brass.

The bulb horn appeared no more, but was replaced by a hand Klaxon with a polished brass belled end. In August the Stewart speedometer was discontinued as standard equipment but was available as an optional item.

1916 Ford Model T

The transitional styling of 1915 remained for 1916, which style year may be considered starting in January.

Types and prices (August)

Touring	Runabout	Town	Sedan	Coupelet
$360	$345	$595	$640	$505

Profits: $59,000,000.

Salient features: After April, all lamps and the horn were entirely black and the engine hood was made of steel.

Bodies

This transitional style was the last to have the semblance of antiquity afforded by the straight front fenders, the small, brass radiator and the little boxlike engine hood, now made of steel instead of aluminum. Later, even the patches of leather on the upholstering at the doors were replaced with leatherette and this was protected from wear by little pressed-steel caps.

Running gear

The 60 in. tread, which required larger fenders, longer fender brackets, longer axles, housings, tie rods and so on, was discontinued after July 31 and Dixieland was compelled at last to superimpose the standard 56 in. tread Fords on their 60 in. ruts.

Hubcaps were still fabricated of thin, polished brass.

1917 Ford Model T

In September 1916, Model T developed a "new look" for 1917. Streamlining came—almost.

Types and prices (August)

Touring	Runabout	Town	Coupelet	Sedan
$360	$345	$595	$505	$646

Profits: $38,500,000. Profits were smaller because of the tremendous building program at the River Rouge plant, subject of the famous Dodge brothers' stockholders suit.

Salient features: High steel radiator shell; larger engine hood matching the cowl contour; crowned, curved fenders; low-compression engine; nickel-plated hub and radiator caps.

Engine

By increasing the height of the cylinder head, engine compression was lowered to 45 psi, with a 3.98:1

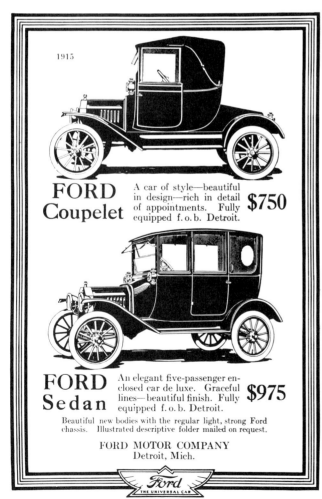

A 1915 Ford ad for the Couplet and Sedan.

24

compression ratio. The cast-iron nozzle for the water hose on top of the cylinder head was increased in length because of the higher radiator. The fan was made larger and had a peripheral reinforcing ring, which was later omitted.

The transmission cover was of cast iron instead of aluminum, and the pedals were smooth-surfaced. Rubber pedal pads were available and could be slipped onto the pedals. The muffler still had cast-iron heads, but the tailpipe was eliminated.

Bodies

A major step was taken this year toward modernizing the Model T. Most striking of all changes was the high, pressed-steel radiator shell with the well-proportioned hood clashed down to pressed-steel sills and fairing gently back to the cowl contour. Crowned fenders were the completing touch. For the first time, nickel plating appeared on the hubcaps and radiator cap. The front bracket holding the body to the frame was then made of a steel stamping rather than the steel casting previously used.

Steering gear

The front-wheel hubs and the spindles were made about ⅛ in. longer, the better to accommodate tapered roller bearings introduced as standard this year. These roller bearings could, however, replace the ball bearings in any earlier models.

A 1917 Coupe with body slightly reminiscent of a horsedrawn carriage.

A 1917 Town Car or Landaulet, sometimes used as a taxi. This was a Model T for those who preferred to have a chauffeur do the driving.

Lamps and accessories

An electric horn powered by the magneto was included as regular equipment this year.

1918 Ford Model T

There was no change from the 1917 to the 1918 style, but starting this year many cars were fitted with squared-end spring leaves, as well as the regular tapered-end spring leaves. For the last time, the Coupelet and Town Cars were offered. Following this year, the Coupe type was revived, having door hinges at the front.

Types and prices (August)

Touring	Runabout	Coupelet	Sedan
$425	$500	$650	$775

1919 Ford Model T

While styling remained identical to 1917, many engineering advances were incorporated in the new Ford for 1919.

Types and prices (August)

Touring	Runabout	Coupe	Sedan
$525	$500	$650	$775

Salient features: First with electric starter and demountable rims as limited optional equipment.

Engine

For the open-type cars, no engine changes *at first* appeared, but for all the closed types, the engine was modified in order to accept the starting equipment as optional equipment. Later, all engines were so modified. The flywheel was altered to take a ring gear. The engine block and (for the fifth time) the timing gear cover were changed to support and drive the 6 volt generator from the camshaft gear, and the transmission cover was redesigned to receive the starting motor.

Because of the generator load on the timing gears, these were changed from spur to helical. This also reduced the backlash and gear noise. The helical gears were interchangeable with the earlier type spur and were recommended by Ford for replacements.

A 1919 center-door Model T.

Bodies

Body styles were not changed from those introduced for 1917, except for reviving the Coupe, which had doors hinged at the front.

Running gear

Demountable clincher rims for 30x3½ tires were optional equipment for the closed-type Fords only. Tire size in front remained 30x4 otherwise. The front radius rods were relocated to a position below the front axle on extensions of the spring perches. This better braced the axle against torque.

Lamps and accessories

All cars fitted with the optional electric starter and battery were also supplied with an electric taillamp, and the 6 volt lighting system, wired in parallel, was powered by the battery. Later, and until the passing of the hand crank and oil taillamp in 1925, the electric taillamp became a popular accessory for those Fords still lighted by the magneto.

1920 Ford Model T

Styling remained unchanged.

Types and prices (March)

Touring	Runabout	Coupe	Sedan
$575	$550	$850	$975

Salient features: Steering wheel was increased to 16 in. diameter.

Engine

Lightweight connecting rods were introduced having a bore of 1⅜ in. with a ¹⁄₁₆ in. of babbitt thickness.

At this time, electric starting became optional on all types at an extra cost of $75, adding 90 lb. extra weight.

The Ford carburetor Model NH was introduced on many cars and Model F carburetor was continued until 1923. Kingston carburetor Model L-2 was discontinued after this year.

Bodies

Bodies remained unchanged from the 1917 style, except that only the Sedan was fitted with a dashboard.

In anticipation of lowered bodies, the original style round fuel tank was abandoned early in 1920 in favor of the oval shape for all body types except the Sedan, which still required the square tank, as used on many of the earlier Coupes.

Steering gear

The familiar cast-steel spider was replaced by a pressed steel unit, and the wheel, now made of "composition" similar to hard rubber, was increased to 16 in. in diameter.

Running gear

At last, optional equipment for all Fords, the demountable rims, including spare, cost $21 extra and added about 70 lb. to the car's weight.

A 1920 center-door Model T, seen at a 1975 Model T gathering at Santa Catalina, California.

Lamps and accessories

The dashboard (Sedan only) sported an ammeter and a combination light and ignition switch mounted in an escutcheon plate. Stewart speedometers, when added, appeared on the lower right edge on the dashboard.

1921 Ford Model T

The style was the same as the 1920 except for minor changes.

Types and prices (June)

Touring	Runabout	Coupe	Sedan
$415	$370	$695	$760

Profits: Ford *owed* $50,000,000 in the postwar depression.

Engine

The front engine support and front spring clamp were forged in one single unit. The pair of U-bolts formerly holding spring to frame were abandoned.

A Kingston carburetor, Model L-4, was furnished on many cars in 1921–22.

1922 Ford Model T

This style was identical to the 1921.

Types and prices

Touring	Runabout	Coupe	Sedan
$348	$319	$580	$645

Bodies

The Sedan with the two centrally located doors and the oval rear window appeared for the last time this year.

1923 Ford Model T

Distinctive, new styling appeared this year in August 1922.

Types and prices

Touring	Runabout	Coupe	two-door	four-door
$393	$364	$530	$595	$725

Profits: $82,000,000.

Salient features: Lowered, more streamlined bodies; one-man top.

Bodies

The lowered bodies, planned since early 1920 when the oval tanks (and the postwar depression) appeared, marked the first real styling advancement since 1917. On all types the radiator was heightened and sported an apron at the bottom of the shell.

Two sedans were offered for the first time, the two-door and the four-door. These and the Coupe featured a large, rectangular rear window and, for the first time, rotary window regulators, a cowl ventilator and, of course, the square fuel tanks.

The Coupe this year had the rear compartment formed integrally with the body. The Runabout still retained the detachable compartment, until the 1926 style, so that it could be readily converted for commercial purposes.

The open-body types had the oval fuel tank, the new one-man top, and windshields set at a rakish angle with the upper section pivoted at the top of the frame. Characteristic of the one-man top was the extension of the back curtain around the side of the bow sockets.

The running board brackets were a one-piece flared channel section and were without the familiar tie rod.

1924 Ford Model T

There were no style changes for 1924.

Types and prices (August)

Touring	Runabout	Coupe	Sedan two-door	Sedan four-door
$295	$265	$525	$590	$685

Profits: $100,000,000 (average $50 per car). Ford started his first nationwide paid advertising program.

Salient features: Last year in which the open cars were available with the 30x3 clincher front tires.

A Danish ad offering the 1922 Model T.

Denne side: Illustration til dansk annonce for Ford-biler, 1922. »Selv den mindste damehånd kan styre en Ford Sedan«, hedder det i annonceteksten — men det ville dog være et særsyn at se damen her befordre de fire kjoleklædte herrer.

SCANIA VABIS - RAADVADDAM
FARVERGADE 17   TLF. 12123 (En-to – En-to-tre)

The NEW FORD "TUDOR" SEDAN

THE Five-Passenger Ford "Tudor" Sedan is suitable for all occasions. It is a car in which one would feel proud to conduct one's friends to social functions or to take one's family on a tour. Comfort and style are the predominant characteristics of this all-season enclosed car. The Ford "Tudor" Sedan is a dignified car, justly appreciated for the perfect finish of its paint work and general refinement. The large plate-glass windows, with mechanical lifts, ensure delightful airiness.

On New Lowered Chassis
Fully equipped with Starter and Lighting Set. Ask your Authorised Dealer for a demonstration run.

Ford

McKenna Duties
Ford Passenger Cars will be reduced in price when these Duties are discontinued. Refund of the whole difference will be made through the Authorised Dealer supplying.

A 1924 English ad for the Model T. Note right-hand steering wheel and mentioning of starter and electric lighting, not seen in 1924 American ads.

1925 Ford Model T

Still in the pattern of 1923, the Ford for 1925 had minor improvements.

Types and prices

Touring	Runabout	Coupe	Tudor Sedan	Fordor Sedan
$290	$260	$520	$580	$660

A 1925 Model T used as a taxi in California. Note the dime fare.

A 1925 ad for the Model T Tudor extolling the virtues of the planetary transmission.

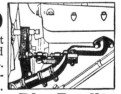

Two 1925 ads for Ford Model T aftermarket water pumps by the same company. Note in the one on the left; a transparent tubing has been inserted in the line to show prospective customers the movement of the water.

Today's High Peak in Motor Car Value

DISPLAY rooms of all Authorized Ford Dealers are thronged with those eager to see the latest Ford body types. Admiration for these attractive cars is expressed everywhere. The low stream-line bodies, the increased roominess, the greater riding comfort and the many convenient new features are advantages which are widely welcomed and appreciated.

Closed cars are finished in attractive colors, with pleasing interior fittings and upholstery to harmonize. The hood and cowl are longer, fenders are larger, wider and more attractive, conforming to the stream-line treatment of the bodies. Rear deck of both the coupe and runabout has a full sweep of line which greatly improves these cars' appearance.

Comfort for driver and passengers has been enhanced by lowering and deepening the seats.

Braking is smoother and more positive, pedals are wider and more conveniently spaced, steering wheel is larger and lower.

Many other important changes and improvements characterize the Ford improved open and closed cars.

The fact that all this has been accomplished without raise in prices is even more impressive than the changes themselves. Ford value, for years holding unchallenged leadership in the motor car market, now reaches a new high peak through the volume and economy of Ford manufacture.

Demand for Ford cars has exceeded all previous records during summer months. Now it is sure to outstrip even the huge production the Ford facilities permit.

FORD MOTOR COMPANY, DETROIT

BEAUTY : : : COMFORT : : : : CONVENIENCE : : : UTILITY

A 1925 Ford praising the car's beauty, comfort, convenience and utility.

Profits: $80,000,000.

Salient features: First with balloon tires and hand-operated windshield wiper.

Bodies

The names Tudor and Fordor were coined to designate the two forms of the Sedan. These names are still used by Ford.

The large black escutcheon plate for the ammeter and the ignition and light switches appeared for the last time on the dashboard. New, as factory equipment, was the hand-operated windshield wiper.

Running gear

Demountable rims for 30x3½ clincher tires were supplied on all body types. The spare was carried at the rear on a triangular mounting. Balloon tires size 4.40x21 were optional equipment for all Fords, at $25 extra.

This was the last year of the small brake drums and the cast-iron brake shoes on the rear wheels.

Lamps and accessories

This was the last year in which open cars were available with no starter, with magneto-powered head lamps and with the same round oil taillamp introduced in 1915 — Ford *did* resist change! Customers still willing to crank preferred, however, to have their Fords fitted with the magneto-powered electric taillamp instead of the oil lamp.

1926 Ford Model T

In a heroic evaluation, Ford brought forth a glamorized Model T for 1926 starting with number 12,225,528 in November 1925. By July 21, 14,000,000 Model T cars had been built.

Types and prices (August)

Touring	Runabout	Coupe	Tudor	Fordor
$380	$360	$485	$495	$545

Profits: $75,000,000.

Salient features: Lowered chassis; nickeled radiator shell; choice of colors; lightweight pistons.

Engine

To help compensate for the heavier bodies, an effort was made to pep up the engine by installing lightweight cast-iron pistons having the oil ring below the wrist pin and by redesigning the intake manifold for more efficient vaporization of fuel.

The engine block casting was altered to provide bosses to which a pair of ears on the new transmission cover could be bolted.

The transmission band was increased in width from 1⅛ to 1¾ in., and all bands were factory-fitted with removable ears to permit relining of bands without removal of the transmission cover. The water nozzle on the engine head had a projection for mounting the fan.

Bodies

After a decade of nothing but black Fords, colors for the closed cars only became optional; blue, grey and brown were offered. This year, the cowl ventilator (introduced in 1923) was included in all cars and served a double duty in that the fuel tank was now located in the cowl and filled through the open ventilator. There was the usual exception: the Fordor had the usual square fuel tank under the seat.

At last, the left front door of the open cars was given hinges and allowed to open, and the Runabout was finally constructed with an integral rear compartment as the Coupe had been in 1923. Running boards were made 1½ in. wider.

Since bodies had been lowered to the practical limit in 1923, these remained essentially unchanged and the height of the Model T was reduced 1½ in. by lowering the chassis. This was accomplished by lowering the crown of the rear spring 1½ in., and by lower-

A 1925 ad extolling the virtues of the 1926 model. Note in this ad that no illustration was used — merely a giant copy of the Ford logo script. Note also the admission that "Closed cars in color" were now available, though no mention was made of the fact that starters and electric lights were now also standard equipment. Perhaps their late introduction prevented Ford from bringing up the subjects.

ing the crown of the front spring 1 in., then gaining the extra ½ in. in front by raising the wheel spindle on the steering-knuckle body. Again, there was an exception: the Tudor body was lowered another 2½ in., for a total of 4 in.

Now proudly displaying a nickel-plated shell, the radiator was ⅝ in. higher. The engine hood was longer, had more louvers and sloped smoothly into the cowl, which appeared to be but a continuation of the hood. In all, the bodies had thus been lengthened 3½ in., and a better sense of proportion was gained by enlarging the crowned fenders and by eliminating the bead on them.

The Coupe and Tudor type only were fitted with a new one-piece windshield, but on all types, the dashboard was furnished with a small nickel-plated escutcheon plate for the ammeter and switches.

Steering gear
The steering-wheel diameter was increased to 17 in. and the planetary-steering gear ratio was changed to 5:1 ratio reduction to compensate for the extra resistance of the balloon tires.

Running gear
Balloon tires, size 4.40x21 were standard equipment on all cars, as were the wooden artillery wheels. This year wire wheels of the drop-center type were available as optional equipment. The spare was mounted at the rear on a tubular post with a flange for the wire wheel or with a three-legged spider for the demountable rim, as required.

The rear-wheel brake drums were increased in diameter from 8 to 11 in. and in width to 1½ in., and the brake shoes were of the asbestos-lined, self-energizing type.

Ignition
The metal spark-coil box was relocated from the dashboard to a bracket on the left side of the engine head.

Lamps
Because of the tubular post, the taillight was relocated from the center of the spare-tire bracket to the left rear fender.

Headlamps had nickel-plated rims and were at first mounted as usual on flange posts. Starting in January 1926, the headlamps were mounted on the front fenders, passing in front of the radiator shell.

1927 Ford Model T
After 19 years, production of Model T cars ended with car number 15,007,033 in June 1927.

Types and prices (June)

Touring	Runabout	Coupe	Tudor	Fordor
$380	$360	$485	$495	$545

Profits: Ford ended the year with a loss of $30,280,000.

Salient features: the 1927 style was identical to 1926, except that only the wire wheels were available. All cars were offered in colors, with maroon and green added.

Chapter 2

My Experiences with the Model T

Floyd Clymer

Tin Lizzie, Flivver, Jitney, Gas Buggy, Henry's Heap, Ford's Jalopy—every joke sold a car

Ford jokes were an endearing and ribtickling kind of humor that infected vaudeville jokes, the masters of ceremonies' speeches at dinner parties, and wherever citizens and fellow townsmen got together. They couldn't resist including a joke about the Ford or the Tin Lizzie in their kit of humor, their stage act or their after-dinner conversation over cigars and brandy. These jokes amused no one more than Henry Ford himself. He often said that every joke sold a Ford Model T car.

One of the advantages of a man with a Ford over the buggy rider with a horse in 1908—the first year the T was offered—was that he could modify his car to plow fields with it on weekends and still go country-riding in it on Sundays. Legions of owners used their Model Ts to saw wood, pump water, store grain, run stock shears, and generate electricity and for other jobs that the most imaginative had never dreamed of before.

Millions of former owners of the Model T still hold the Lizzie in affectionate esteem. For the Ford, beside guaranteeing a ride through snow and rain, was also a means for the go-getter to increase his sales and the doctor to do his calling, and all in all contributed more than any other car to welding together towns and cities of this country. The Model T, although it was to share the American market with approximately 2,200 other makes of cars, was an automobile that helped to revolutionize a people's way of life. Ford's jalopy, as the "common man's car," was a unique contributor to the history of transportation in America.

Exactly what sort of contraption was this car? First of all, it was a car of contradictions. It was imperfect, and its imperfections were a part of its fascination. Sometimes she wouldn't start on cold mornings, or she burned too much oil, or she got poor mileage

A 1915 ad for "Funny Ford Stories."

"Do you have to drive into town today, Ma? I was planning on using the car for plowin' the north twenty."

over the muddy roads, or she wouldn't outrun a jack rabbit. And once started, would the engine keep running? One farmer even vowed that the potatoes on a piece of his hilly farm land could hold her back. The blamed thing was always the subject of complaints. These became the fertile soil for the accessory manufacturers who, over the twenty years of the Model T's life, were to turn out some 5,000 gadgets to dress up and cause to run "with the surest ease and invincible power" that rattling T that stood out in the woodshed.

For many years the Model T came equipped with only the barest necessities—no speedometer or starter, no temperature gauges or bumpers. And even though Ford was one of the first manufacturers to place the steering wheel on the left side, steering the T was a whole lot like driving a truck—or at least so said many complaining flivver owners.

The Model T, however, was supposed to be the latest word in automotive engineering. It took you just where you wanted to go. Parts were cheap and available in almost any small town or farmer's barn, and if

you could drive it, you could fix it yourself. That was real designing. And with his use of vanadium steel, Henry Ford succeeded in building a quality and dependability into his car which many other higher-priced cars did not possess.

In the early scramble for sales in the automotive field, many salesmen and representatives for a tire-puller or tractor-attachment firm drove Model Ts. Furthermore, speaking in a mechanical jargon, the salesman would take out your clutch before your very eyes to show you that his tool kit for the clutch and other related parts on the Model T was the best on the market. The greater part of Ford owners at one time or another tinkered with their cars, removed a transmission band here, cleaned the spark plugs there, greased, hammered, wiped and pampered. They were a high-spirited bunch, forever talking about their Ts.

They learned of necessity how to repair their own cars. They represented the mechanical America that was on its way. It was easy enough to exchange the brake bands, or take off the head and the pan to put in a new piston. Because there were so few mechanics as we know them these days, situated on every corner in our cities, the man who owned a Ford then often did most of the mechanical work himself. The motorist accepted his roadside grief with his joy. For this reason, Ford had more dealers by far than did any other maker.

The driver of this top-heavy jalopy knew, too, when his T was hitting on three instead of four cylinders. Many a car owner today can't tell whether his V-8 is hitting on seven or eight. And if you were to suggest that he clean his spark plugs, he might throw up his hands in helplessness. His auto is a piece of precision machinery, a far cry from the Model T. That is one reason for the average motorist's disinterest in his car's engine. He feels that he could not possibly understand it.

But the fact of the matter is people today would rather let George do it. Neither could they repair their engines, nor do they care much about how they work. That is evolution. Yet it is hard to forget the days when, to survive on the road, a man had to be a mechanic. He had to get out and get under, if he wanted to put his car back on the road. Ford dealers prospered in that do-it-yourself climate.

At the tender age of eleven, I was a dealer for Reo, Maxwell and Cadillac cars in the little town of Berthoud, fifty miles north of Denver. In two years of hard bargaining, I sold twenty-six cars. Ford was not very stout competition then. I had been selling one-cylinder Reos, two-cylinder Maxwells and one-cylinder Cadillacs. But four cylinders, for $500, although a considerable sum, was a recognizable bargain that began to make a dent in my sales. My little one-cylinder Cadillac was selling for $750.

A 1923 ad detailing the advantages of the Kirstin Fil-O-Meter method of filling the Model T gas tank.

I'll never forget the day I met Henry Ford. It was in 1907 in Denver when a Ford salesman, who later became one of Ford's closest friends and manager of Ford's Denver assembly plant, introduced me to the car builder. Mr. Hendy, the salesman, told Ford I was the youngest car dealer in the world. "Some day I hope you will be selling Fords," Mr. Ford said to me. I met him several times after that and he always remembered me as that young car salesman out West.

It was not until 1908 that the land-office Model T business began to starch up the sales in my district. The local Ford dealer was a fellow named George Nall and he naturally drove a Model T. That T of George's was some machine. When it got a leak in the radiator, which was quite often, he would put a handful of oatmeal or cornmeal in it to plug up the leak, at least temporarily. He was trying to do the same thing with my car sales, and it was plenty hard to keep up with him.

George was so enterprising in those days that he even went in for taking trade-ins. He'd take a horse and buggy from a prospective customer or allow him a generous discount on a Model T.

In those days, a man needed only to buy a manufacturer's car and, if the territory was open, he could have the dealership thrown in. That was the situation around Berthoud. I had run up some sizeable profits selling one- and two-cylinder cars at prices higher than what the four-cylinder T sold for. Ford's flivver, at that low price, seemed just short of sensational when it first appeared.

In order to meet this new competition, I flushed the farmers' sugar-beet and wheat fields and the Main Street stores for new buyers. Then I took on the EMF 30 and, a few months later, the Flanders 20, both built by EMF in Detroit and distributed by Studebaker, the

wagon people in South Bend, Indiana. They were fair sellers, good hard-rock bargains in looks, dependability and savings in boot wear.

The first Model T, if it lacked elegant style and mohair cushions, did boast improvements over the earlier Ford models, as well as competitors' makes of cars. A mysterious howling, jerking mechanism, called the planetary transmission, came installed on the 1908 T. It was all enclosed except for the sound and, with two speeds forward and a reverse, it was the epitome of gearboxes of its day. If the planetary was cranky and anything but quiet, it still made motoring a sport. Only when the 1928 Model A appeared, equipped with sliding gears, did T drivers—some grieved, others relieved—realize that Ford had abandoned his famous gear scramble called the planetary.

One of the 1908 Model T improvements was the steering wheel and wobbly column on the lefthand

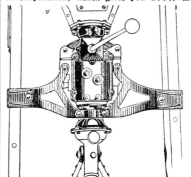

"We'll give you more trade-in for your old horse and buggy than any other dealer in town."

A 1920 ad for a most interesting offer for Model T owners—installing a Chevrolet transmission, in combination with the standard epicyclic original, which "gives you 100% more power."

side. A few of the off-brand models before the Model T had lefthand steering, but Ford was the first manufacturer of any consequence to stick the driver in the left front seat in order to accommodate the ladies and oncoming traffic. Passengers could climb down off the high leather seats onto the board sidewalk, instead of the gumbo of the mud street. And it was possible for two lonely motorists, way out in the country, twenty miles from home, to pull their jalopies together alongside each other and inquire as to weather and road conditions and a "Have you a patch or two you can spare, brother?"

There were certain other notable features about the 1908 Model T flivver. The engine had a low-tension magneto built into the flywheel. The timer and coils gave plenty of trouble, as did the oil line, which had a habit of becoming clogged. Many inventions appeared on the market designed for cleaning the line once it had become plugged up. The new flivver was cooled by the thermosyphon system rather than by water pump. (Editor's note: The first 2,500 Model Ts actually had a water pump.) Ford did continue to use the

transverse spring suspension of his former models, both front and rear. The drive shaft was enclosed, and the Model T had radius rods from the rear axle to the rear of the transmission and from the engine to the front axle. Henry cast his four-cylinder 20 hp engine *en bloc* on his Tin Lizzie, instead of in pairs, as had been done on previous Fords.

Any blacksmith or Model T owner knew about the improved engine. George Nall was an expert when it came to the Model T. He was more than just a salesman. Even though we were competitors, we were friends. Intrigued by the new Model T, I took many a ride in it with him into the country, where he explained the car's fine points to me. Even then I admired the new car that was just then beginning to be called the flivver. Also about this time, the word jitney was coined, probably because so many Model Ts were being used in rental services.

I remember one extremely cold morning when we started on a short trip to Loveland in George's demonstrator. Six miles of snow-covered road lay ahead and the temperature had dropped below zero. George had put antifreeze in the radiator, a homemade solution of alcohol and water. The Model T was notoriously hard to start on cold mornings, but George had learned that if he jacked up one of the rear wheels, released the handbrake and gave the crank a few turns, it would start more readily. We went through this ritual that

A blowtorch to heat the intake manifold, a bucket of boiling water and a strong arm always helped a Model T owner get going on a cold winter morning.

morning, but his demonstrator was balky and still refused to start.

George had plenty of Model T savvy. The proper manner of starting the T was to crank the engine, using the battery ignition first, and once the engine started, flip the switch to ignition by magneto, or "mag" as it was commonly called. My ingenious friend put a kettle of water on the kitchen stove. Meantime, he drained the radiator. When the water came to a boil, he unscrewed the radiator cap and poured in the hot water. I can still hear the crackling sound as the hot water hit the ice-cold metal of the cylinder block. Once the engine was started and the rear wheel was once again on the ground, the car crept forward slowly and almost crushed George between the radiator and the wall of the barn that was his garage. George was not always light of foot.

One of the quirks of "Henry's Heap," as some called the car, on those cold mornings when there seemed to be no life in her, was that the T had the "creeps." Many is the time I cranked and pulled out the carburetor choke and then reset the hand spark and throttle levers and cranked again. Usually the engine would commence to hit on two or three cylinders, then cough and break out in a glorious, deafening roar. She would really sound sweet—like a thresher trimming the nap off an acre of barbed wire. But when she shook and shivered and was running, she also had a tendency to crawl forward, so that I had to put both hands on the radiator and push until I could make a dash for the front seat to adjust the spark and gas levers before the engine conked out. The throttle lever was located under the steering wheel; until a few gadget makers offered one, the Model T had no foot throttle.

The Model T was a car that rared to go, a challenge to every driver. Once the engine had run for a few minutes and the crankcase oil was warmed up, the car settled down; and there never was, in the twenty years of its life, a finer piece of automotive machinery, as dependable as a pack mule if you carried a tool kit and checked her gas regularly. And I never can recall my friend George taking a horse and buggy out of town to bring back his Model T.

I can still recall how George taught me to check the oil. There was no dipstick in those days. I got down on my knees and, with a pair of pliers, turned one of the two petcocks located in the lower half of the flywheel housing. If oil ran out of the top petcock, the oil supply was OK. If no oil came out of the lower petcock, we were headed straight for bearing trouble if oil was not added—pronto! This was a primitive method of testing the oil supply, but any ten-year-old kid could learn how to do it.

Returning from that same trip to Loveland that day, we journeyed through some hilly country west of town and found the Model T demo climbed nearly every grade without too much difficulty. We ran into one hill, though, where she sputtered and almost stopped. George knew right away what the trouble was. With the gas tank under the seat, the gravity flow of the gas to the carburetor wasn't working properly. Equal to the emergency, he swung the car around, so that we headed down hill, then backed up the hill!

Indeed, many folks claimed that the Model T worked better in reverse than in low gear on a sharp grade, and doubtless this quirk of the gravity fuel sys-

"Help!"

"Hey, George. She needs a little oil."

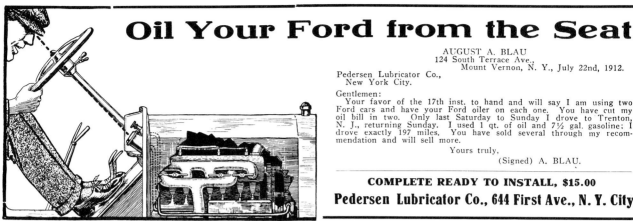

A 1912 ad for a device to locate an oil gauge on the dash of the Model T.

tem was what they referred to. The gravity flow was positive and constant in hill backing. Also, the gear ratio for reverse was lower than for the low forward gear, and this gave the car added power.

I recall a similar event that took place outside of Berthoud in those few years before the Model T had caught on. There was a fast-talking old farmer in the area who had taken to the "gas buggy" and was dealing out Fords for Henry. One of his neighboring farmers was looking for just the right automobile, and the old codger proceeded to give his friend and prospective buyer a demonstration. The prospective buyer had heard down at the barber shop that several drivers,

gripping their wheels for dear life, had tried to crawl up a steep quarter-mile of hill from the road to his house.

He promised to buy a Ford if he could be shown that it would climb the hill. "Be glad to," said the farmer-salesman, and he started up the hill, the customer alongside of him in the front seat and hanging onto a top strut. The jalopy did fine until about halfway up the hill when it began to buck and cough. The quick-witted salesman swung the steering wheel over and into a side road. Then he pushed the reverse pedal and backed into the road again, remarking with great pride, "You see, this hill is really nothing. I can even back up it!"

At the top of the hill, the buyer, in great wonderment, signed the order. The salesman had some tall explaining to do, however, when the irate owner later

"Look! I can even back up this hill!"

"I understand he can afford a new car, only he doesn't want to give up his mother-in-law seat on his 1909 model."

found that he could not pull the entire quarter-mile in low gear. For over a year, that farmer had to back up the last 200 yards to his house. Soon he got the hang of it, though, and was boasting to his friends about sighting along the post fence and scrub oak for accurate back-up aim.

In 1909, Ford brought out a slick roadster. It was one of the most unusual models in the whole Ford line, made so by the one-passenger bucket seat in the rear, completely exposed to the weather. This remarkable commode, shaped like a bucket half, was often referred to as the mother-in-law seat. Also in 1909, Ford mounted a brass gas generator on the running board, and by the use of the carbide gas it generated, furnished gas for the lights.

Water, carried in the upper part of the generator, would drop onto lumps of carbide, and the acetylene gas so formed would flow through rubber or copper tubing to the headlights. Kerosene cowl lights and taillights — and bulb horn — were kept highly polished and were pointed out with pride by the Model T owner. With lights, the city-bound man could drive at night, and when he squeezed the bulb horn, a raucous blast would inform other drivers and pedestrians of his presence.

That year, too, Ford made much to-do about his use of vanadium steel in some high-stress parts, espe-cially axles. For years, his advertising and dealer displays played up that feature, often showing a vanadium-steel axle twisted like a pretzel but unbroken, to prove the toughness of the material.

By 1910, the Model T Ford was on the upswing in popularity, gaining more customers every day over my EMF and Flanders. I was, in fact, losing loyal customers simply because the Ford was a cheaper car. Though the EMF factory was producing in the Flanders a fast, stylish machine in the low-priced field, repair and operation costs were not on a thrifty par with the Model Ts.

The Ford owner had clincher tires and no spare. He always carried a spare tube and a tire-repair outfit. Sometimes he strapped an extra tire casing on the rear, on the side or over the hood for a long journey. This was one of the many ways the Ford owner could save on tires. But the true dyed-in-the-wool flivver man needed only to say he drove a "plain jalopy and bought two gallons of gas three days ago" to convince many folks away from my cars. Ford, as a product and a name, was becoming a byword, as native to the American scene as Boston baked beans and Georgia grits and gravy.

Henry Ford, too, was becoming a well-known figure. By repute, he was a stubborn and independent man who built the car he felt most like building. He

A two-ton hay load on a Model T and trailer, showing the extreme versatility of the T.

claimed, and sincerely believed, that his Model T was the car people ought to own. In a few years—1913, to be exact—he was to advertise a cure for insomnia with the slogan: "Open your eyes and watch the Fords go by."

The Ford owner swore by his car, as well as at it. The Model T's success in the first half-dozen years of its existence was due partly to the temper of the day and the desires of the motorist. The following is a good example of the exuberance with which many people truly admired, bought and drove their Ts. This ad, which appeared in the early *Ford Times*, a propaganda publication if one ever existed, spoke for the exuberant consumer as well as the producer.

"It leads the way; it blazes the trail; it sets the pace. To the utmost corners of the earth the Ford journeys. It is the pioneer car in many lands. Many sections of the Canadian Northwest knew no other car but the Ford. The first car on the island of Jolo was a Ford. A Ford was the first to scale Scotland's Ben Nevis. The first pleasure car across the Gobi desert in Mongolia was a Ford town car destined for the living God of Urga. Even here in the United States, there are many places where Ford has led the way for the rest. It has been the first automobile owned in the country, the first to cause pride to the village, the first to traverse the rough trail. . . ."

Late in 1910, I decided that if I was ever to get anywhere in the car business, I had better join up with a fast-moving company to sell a make whose popularity had staggered the lovers of quiet and the connoisseurs of the horse and buggy. The Model T Ford, I felt, would be a rich vein. With little trouble, I secured a job selling Fords for a couple of brothers in Walla Walla. Harold Dahlen, a former lumberman from Belling-

ham, Washington, had just opened a Ford agency in town with his brother. Three or four other Ford agencies had failed in Walla Walla. But these agencies had sold earlier model Fords, the N, the R, the S and the K but no Model Ts.

I helped Dahlen unload from the boxcar the first railroad shipment of Ts to come to Walla Walla. In the face of buyers' bias and their disgruntlement over previous Ford models, we had to pitch a strenuous line of sales chatter. By dint of local ads and repeated personal calls, we managed to sell all but one of the seven cars in the first carload. The last model was a coupe. It stood on the showroom floor for at least six months. Nobody wanted to ride in a coupe, at the risk of getting diced up by glass and roof posts in that accident that was sure to happen.

Despite hometown resistance to the coupe and to the T model generally, people who owned the T and drove it, liked it. Meanwhile, I kept a sharp eye out for a sale and a motoring trip. In those days there were traveling stock companies, playing in the small, out-of-the-way towns in the Midwest and Far West. Dahlen was a liberal man and he furnished me with a Model T demo. One afternoon, when a troupe of actors and actresses, playing in a local stock company, came around to the store and asked me for a ride in a T, without Dahlen's authorization, I loaded them into my jalopy and we went out for the country.

We were bumping along fine on a long stretch of Washington's straw-covered dusty road. The throttle

"I don't care if you do like the pretty posies, Mandy. I'm not going to take a chance on us getting all cut up when that 'glass showcase' turns over on us!"

"She don't run so hot when you hit a deep rut, I'll admit."

was wide open; about 40 miles per hour was a good top speed in the old T. I reached over to lean up the mixture by turning a knob extending through the cowl on the righthand side; the knob controlled the adjustment of the carburetor needle valve. At the same instant I took my hand off the wheel, the car struck a deep rut, crossed the road and plowed into a ditch.

It rolled over and over before coming to a stop. One of the actors suffered a broken arm, another a broken leg, and all of us were skinned and bruised. One had a bloody nose and his pants were torn off. My only injury resulted from the back of the seat roughing up the nape of my neck. As for the car, the fenders were crumpled, the top bashed in, windshield folded, glass broken and the upholstery torn loose. My T demonstrator was ready for the scrap heap!

Mr. Dahlen considered the ride a "joy ride" instead of a demonstration. He was ready to fire me but finally decided against it, in order to protect his investment. I was to pay him back for the damages out of my $12 a week salary and $5 per-car commission. Although it wasn't easy to pay for an almost completely wrecked Model T when they were selling for $700, I scraped together and borrowed enough money to pay off my debt in a year's time. In nearly fifty years of motoring, this was my only serious accident.

Competitive makes of cars were vying against each other in endurance, speed and performance contests. The Northwest was considered one of the badlands spots for automobiles. At about this time, I witnessed an interesting hill-climbing contest between a Ford and an air-cooled Franklin.

The race was up a long, winding hill in the Blue Mountains of southwestern Washington, not far from our town of Walla Walla. R. P. Rice, then manager of the Ford branch in Seattle, sat at the wheel of a stripped-down Model T that day and, as the car curled up the mountain leaving the dust flying under its wheels, he really brought out the heart in that little flivver. The crowd was scattered along the length of the race hill and, much to their amazement, they saw the popular big air-cooled Franklin fall behind Mr. Rice's T on top of the hill, an easy winner.

In order to push sales, Ford never failed to editorialize on the fact that his model T could often outperform larger, heavier and more expensive cars. Through his advertising and cartoons, which the motorist could find in the lobby of the remotest hotel in the smallest American town, he acquainted the public with the car with a unit powerplant type of engine with a mind of its own.

One such ad in 1913 showed the earth as seen by Martians; the earth is ringed, like Saturn, but by Model T Fords! Another cartoon the same year showed a big car, stalled on a stubborn hill, being

pushed by sweating men and being pulled by a team of straining plow horses. Nearby, a gay foursome, in an open Model T, airily whiz up the hill. The caption reads "Too big."

In a way, such exuberant ads and cartoons, coupled with my personal experiences with the Model T, helped sway me in one direction. About 1911, the family returned to Colorado, and, seeing with my own eyes that Fords were gaining in sales on other makes of cars, I decided to devote my energies to selling Henry's Model T. The branch manager of the Denver Ford Motor Company was still the same Charles K.

Even the Martians could see the Ford's popularity.

Portions of a 1913 ad of the Ford Motor Company with a cartoon basis. They apparently proved quite popular.

41

"Doc, if it's a boy, I'm going to name him Henry. If it's a girl, I'm going to name her Lizzie."

siderable beating around the bush, for the plain fact of the matter was that Ford factory officials at Dearborn did not approve of a sixteen-year-old kid selling their cars. I had to settle for a job selling Model Ts as a sort of curbstone broker.

The man I principally sold Model Ts for, Jim Lanham, was pretty strict about my using his flivvers for other purposes than demonstrating. But he did not blame me for one "errand of mercy" that I did for my father, Dr. J. B. Clymer, a small-town physician and surgeon for forty years. One morning Dad rushed over to the Lanham garage with the news that his two-cylinder Maxwell was balky and that he was urgently needed at the Jackson farm ten miles out to deliver a baby.

He hopped in my T demonstrator and we rattled out to the farm. Dad decided to try to get Mrs. Jackson to the hospital, so we piled back into the car, the nervous expectant father and I in the front seat, Dad and Mrs. Jackson in the back. I had driven half way back to Loveland, trying to avoid the bigger bumps and ruts, when Dad suddenly ordered me to pull over to the side of the road and told me to sit on the running board and put my hands over my ears. I did manage to hear Mr. Jackson swear to name the child "Henry if he's a boy, Lizzie if she's a girl." A few minutes later, Dad deliv-

Hendy who had introduced me to Mr. Ford in 1907. With Mr. Hendy's help, I signed up to handle Fords in Louisville, Colorado. There was some delay and con-

"Hey, Lew, I knew you'd run out of steam. Next time, get a Ford!"

ered a sturdy boy and Mr. Jackson kept his promise.

Not long after this incident, a prospective car buyer who enjoyed a good argument said he would buy a Model T or a Stanley Steamer, whichever could win a road race from Loveland to Greeley—a distance of twenty-two miles. The following Sunday morning, two cars lined up for the race. I was driving a Model T and Lew Hertha, a 20 hp Stanley Steamer. Word of the race spread quickly and some 500 people gathered at the start of the race and an equal number at the city limits of Greeley to see the finish.

The straight road ahead of us was dry and dusty, and at the start, the Stanley left me far back in her dust. Driving the Model T wide open in hot pursuit, even over the chuckholes and deep ruts, I managed a speed of about 45 miles an hour. Gradually I started to gain on the Stanley and about five miles from Greeley, Lew began to slow down. I drew closer, and finally came alongside, well aware of the fact that Lew's steam was running low. Lew had a disappointed look on his face as he tried to build up his steam pressure.

As I neared the finish line, he was gaining fast, but his pressure didn't rise quickly enough and I beat him across the finish line by about 200 feet. Mr. Lanham gave me an extra $10 bonus for making the sale—or was it for beating the Stanley?

In the early days of the automobile business, it was not unusual for car dealers to take horsedrawn vehicles, a horse or team of horses, a cow or pig, or occasionally even farm machinery in trade, as part payment, on a new car. In a small farming community it was often customary to take all kinds of products to make a sale.

I had made a few such deals, and had been told by Mr. Lanham that he couldn't use any more livestock during that particular month. But a farmer named Oscar Johnson who lived about five miles out in the country said he would buy a Model T if we would take his two-cylinder Maxwell, a horse and a bicycle which his son had outgrown in trade as part payment. Always the eager salesman, I decided to take a chance and made the deal on the spot, knowing that I could at least sell the Maxwell easily. The trip back to Loveland was made slowly in low gear, with the horse tied back of the Maxwell. I was counting on the local auctioneer to sell the horse, the Maxwell and probably the bicycle as well at his auction the next day. When I drove up to the garage in the Maxwell, Jim Lanham was mad as a wet hen.

He didn't mind so much about the Maxwell but that old nag really upset him, and when he saw the bicycle, he nearly blew a fuse. At first he was going to fire me but when auctioneer Warnock got more for the horse, the Maxwell and the bicycle than I had allowed

"I told you, no more livestock this month, Floyd!"

A 1924 ad for a gas tank which makes it "impossible to drain the tank completely" preventing running out of gas. Unusual in that it is not another tank, "just a valve anyone can install in five minutes" to the standard tank.

Mr. Johnson, he cooled off considerably. In fact, he gave me an extra $5 commission for the sale.

Most drivers needed a gas gauge but the T had none. As a result, it was standard practice for the flivver to run out of gas about five miles from the nearest gas station. Instructions were that the driver should cross the field to the farmer's house. His only option was—which farmhouse? He should then hope against hope that in the middle of the night the farmer would have a can of gasoline on the premises, or a telephone for calling home. If he was really stuck and the sun hadn't gone down, the motorist could stand beside his car along the deserted road and wait until the next infrequent motorist came along. The latter, with a knowing glance, would be prepared to siphon a little gas out of his tank for him.

To forestall these emergencies, a motorist could buy several different kinds of gas savers and even se-

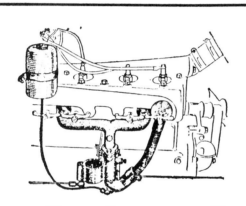

Save Ten Cents on Every Gallon of Fuel

The NITRO solves the high cost of fuel problem which is facing every Ford owner. This new idea in carburetors permits the use of a mixture of kerosene and gasoline—half and half of each.

This results in a saving of at least ten cents per gallon of fuel. Besides that the NITRO furnishes greater power and a smoother running motor than when you use pure gasoline.

The NITRO has been tested by thousands of Ford owners and in every case it has brought about an economy in fuel consumption heretofore unknown.

FORD OWNERS:—Your dealer should have the NITRO in stock ready for installation. If he does not carry it, however, write to us direct for information.

Sunderman Corporation
Newburgh, N. Y.

One of the few dual-fuel arrangements found for the Model T—unusual in that this is not a switch-over to kerosene but a device to burn a half-and-half mix. Note also the device was obtainable from "Your (Ford) dealer."

lect from as many as fifty different kinds of gas gauges, all made by outside firms, of course. (Editor's note: There were many more oil gauges offered by these firms than gas gauges). One such gauge sounded a bell under the seat when the gas supply was low. The flivver driver, of course, had the black ruler supplied by the car agency to stick in the gas tank and measure the gas that was left. Some such sticks were made up by enterprising merchants and carried their ads, not a bad idea at that. The only trouble was, these rulers were easy to lose.

I recall one instance of running out of gas when I was driving a Model T. I went to a farmhouse, but the owner had no gas! He did have a gallon of kerosene—"coal oil" they called it then—in a can with a potato stuck in the spout. Making the best of the situation, I rushed back to the car and emptied the kerosene into my tank. I managed to reach town with the mixture of kerosene and what gasoline fumes were in the carburetor system. The only thing was, a haze of blue smoke kept pouring out of my exhaust as I drove along. The use of kerosene could only be successful if the engine was hot and by spinning to start the engine. A driver had to keep the engine "speeded up" or running fast for the kerosene to work. (Editor's note: Some manufacturers offered "dual fuel" carburetors, especially for the Fordson tractor.)

Along with this out-of-gas inconvenience came another that Model T owners will always associate with this car. The gas tank and cap were under the front seat, so that if a fellow was out with his best girl, he had to ask her apologetically if she would please get out for a minute because they needed gas. This was one of the commonplace scenes of Sunday driving: driver and passenger climbing out of the car so that the gas tank could be filled.

To crank the engine and get it started again could also be a cooperative affair. Mabel sometimes learned how to work the spark and gas levers for her boyfriend. Fords were temperamental, and if the young man had just the right touch, he could tell by the feel of the "innards" and almost by ear just how the engine was perking. And if he was smart, he never wrapped his thumb around the crank. Because of the frequent "kickbacks," it required a light touch to avoid the sprained wrist and skinned knuckles.

In the mid-twenties, a ratchet-type non-kick device was put on the market which disconnected the crank from the engine shaft after the engine fired. Even more interesting was the manually operated starter. It typified the length which some car owners went to put their cars in an up-to-date shape for the new motoring year.

The Hunter Starter ($10) was a clever item that looked like a Rube Goldberg invention. It turned the engine over quickly by a chain operating from a combination of levers which finally ended up in the car, with a handle located within reach of the driver. All he needed to do was pull the handle. Sometimes it actually worked.

A Buffalo, New York, firm put out an electric starter for the Model T. At about that time, 1913–15, the electric starter became generally popular, and with the electric starter came the storage battery.

Around the middle of the decade, the Model T came equipped with electric headlights, although the old kerosene sidelamps mounted on the dashboard were still factory equipment. When the T driver slowed down, the headlights would dim and flicker. Sometimes he preferred to drive in low gear with a fast-turning engine. Then he could read the signs and see the ruts and chuckholes, saving his springs and tires a beating and wear.

The car actually sold itself, however, and at prices that were then unbelievable. For example, the Ford Runabout of 1916 could be had for $390 and the elaborate Sedan for $740. But Ford stated stubbornly and specifically that no speedometer came with these cars, otherwise fully equipped. And if his factory furnished a full set of tools, it ignored the sales possibilities in offering a variety of colors. His 1916 catalog read: "No option is given on color, tires, or equipment." In other words, "Take it or leave it." And Henry Ford made millions of Americans take it and like it.

As early as 1913, though the automobile business was still in its infancy, the high-pressure sales psychology had developed to the point where the company's sales manager, N. A. Hawkins, prophesied that the sales of Fords must increase substantially every year. He claimed that fully two million families needed Fords that year, and he cited the reasons for their need: picnics, road comfort, sales in circuit riding and telephone testing, pleasure and general utility. "At the rate of two million yearly," he concluded, "ten years would be consumed supplying those who already need and have not bought." It was heady talk, but the most optimistic estimate of future business turned out to be the most accurate.

To illustrate the power of his entrenched position in 1914, Ford devised one of the greatest sales promotion stunts in automobile history. On July 31 of that year, he offered a $50 rebate to every Ford buyer, if sales during the following year topped 300,000. The year's total was 308,218, and accordingly $15,410,650 was mailed out to Ford buyers. That was probably one of the first instances of profit sharing under our capitalistic system.

The Hunter starter of 1920. Note the interesting claims for this mechanical-type starter.

A 1917 ad for "bright lights at all speeds" for your Model T. This ad "guaranteed" illumination with only one light, even though the T used headlights in series.

Ford's T had reached the crest of its popularity. His Couplet was one of the best bargains in 1916, and signified Ford values. Wrapped up in one package, here was an "all-year-around" car for two passengers. Ford ads stated that with the top raised, the driver had a "snug, comfortable, enclosed car," and with the top rolled — an effortless two-minute job — he had a "runabout of distinctive appearance." I remember the Couplet for its sleek lines and its gleaming paint and brass finish. If you had $590 for a car, you could buy this dandy right off the showroom floor.

On the 1920 models, Ford made styling and equipment changes that showed automotive progress. The kerosene dashboard lamps were gone. The angular look of the hood was streamlined and, being higher, blended in with the body top. The radiator sat inside of a shell and the front fenders were rounded over the wheels. Ford's Fordor Model T of 1922 was a splendid all-enclosed car for its day. It was powered by an improved four-cylinder 20 hp engine, and if the driver fully opened the accelerator and leaned up the mixture just a bit, he could get 45 miles an hour out of it.

Ten gallons, or a full tank, would take him almost anywhere he wanted to go. A joke of the time put this T economy in a pithy way.

Filling station man: "Yer car needs gas, Mister."

Mr. Grouch (who has stopped for free air): "Say, that flivver had five gallons of gas day before yesterday, and that's every darn drop it's going to get until tomorrow."

The following year Ford turned out an all-enclosed Model T with new styling. Probably the most outstanding features were its low, straight roofline, high radiator and a large oblong windshield that offered maximum visibility. On the practical side, in one hour, if the motorist didn't pinch the tube or mind barking his hands, he could buff up and patch his tube on the front fender, allowing another ten minutes for pumping up the tire with the hand pump.

In 1924 Ford offered what his ad called a "jazzy runabout," a trim Roadster with the same standard four-cylinder, 20 hp engine capable of the usual T speed. This was one of the last radically new body styles in the Model T line. Although the 1926 Touring Car met with great popularity, the Model T was nearing the end of its day. The Touring Car had steel-wire-spoke wheels, but only two-wheel brakes. Though most other makes had changed over to four-wheel brakes, Ford was still adamant against the use of brakes on the front wheels. He contended that they weren't practical. Their upkeep was too costly, they were dangerous because they grabbed, and most useless on the road, from an engineering point of view. No Model T ever had four-wheel brakes; the first Ford car to have them was the 1928 Model A.

In 1927, Ford made one last big effort to keep the Model T on the road. With the gas tank back of the hood and with balloon tires as standard equipment, he offered a choice of colors and gave the customers wire-spoke wheels. He was still convinced, however, that the planetary transmission and two-wheel brakes were what the mass motorists ought to have.

Adults of the twenties who knew their stuff when it came to driving a car more than likely had first learned on Henry's three-pedal Model T. (Editor's note: The first 1,000 Model Ts had two pedals. Reverse was by a lever. This group was later offered a factory kit to modify these earlier models to three pedals.)

When the avalanche of new makes appeared in those exciting days of prosperity, those who had grown up with the Tin Lizzie were having to change their method of shifting the gears in their new cars.

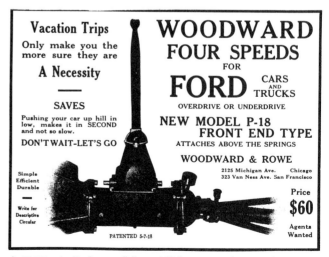

"You mean, I was really doing sixty, officer? How could I tell, without a speedometer?"

A 1918 ad offering a sliding-shift four-speed transmission for the Model T.

Chevrolet, Studebaker, Buick, Dodge Brothers and other makes already had three-speed standard transmissions. Although Henry clung to his two-speed planetary transmission, accessory manufacturers were offering three-speed transmissions to the new Ford owners.

I've got a hunch that Henry might smile a bit if he could look over today's automatic transmissions, which basically employ the old planetary gears he used for so long. He might even say "I told you so." Today, the bands of the planetary unit are operated by hydraulic oil pressure instead of manually, but the principle is essentially the same.

One might suppose from the innumerable gadgets and accessories developed for use on the Model T that owners of the flivver were constantly dissatisfied with their cars. Such was not the case. But the enterprising T owner yearned to improve his car, make it special in some way, add to the quality of its performance and appearance. Nothing was sacred. Lights, cylinder heads, radiators, bodies, bumpers, tops, fenders, windshields—all were manufactured especially for the Model T by independent firms. The accessory makers did not confine themselves to superficial contributions to the Model T. They made new and different parts for the engine, brake and clutch systems, wheels and axles.

Like millions of other Model T owners, I had my eye peeled for the latest products listed and illustrated in the fascinating Auto Accessories sections of the mail-order catalogs. No Ford owner's home was complete without one. Maybe he wanted to buy a set of tire chains or some other cold-weather starting equipment. If his car was an earlier model, he wanted to bring it up to snuff. If he had just purchased the car, he wanted to make a few creative additions.

And so began the hunt for the right gadget. Ultimately, some 5,000 accessories for the Model T Ford appeared on the market. These devices were always made by outside firms, never connected with the Ford Motor Company.

Racing bodies were much in vogue in the early days of the speed mania, around 1913. Remo put out a Raceabout Body, "made as a body should be made," positively the classiest substitute body ever made for the Model T. Arrow advertised that their racing body for $69 "is primarily for a red-blooded man who wants

An actual air spring for the Model T, offered in 1924.

Q.E.D. Spring Oilers were claimed to obviate the need for actual shocks with its means of oiling springs.

NOTICE TO USER

To obtain best Results this car should not be driven faster than 20 miles per hour for the first 500 miles.

Oil should be changed after first 400 miles and every 750 miles thereafter.

IMPORTANT

Always insist on genuine Ford Parts

This note was placed on the windshield of every early Model T before it left the factory. Note the suggestion to use only "genuine Ford parts" for replacements. This was as far as Ford went in admitting that there were other replacement parts.

style and distinctive snap, yet with no sacrifice of comfort."

Dozens of accessory firms proclaimed in the ads that the Model T drove like a truck and rode like a wagon, and that for a small sum, the motorist could acquire Pullman-like comfort with so-and-so's vital-life shock absorbers. Snubbers sold for around $15 for four and were guaranteed "to keep you on the seat."

There were cowl ventilators, a "gasophone" gas gauge with a warning bell and a special gas "filler" which allowed the gas tank to be filled without lifting the seat cushion. All kinds of quick-change transmission bands and new types of braking systems appeared on the market. The T used internal expanding brakeshoes, but some accessory makers invented a rig that added external contracting brakes for extra braking power—something that all Fords needed, not only the Model T.

Most Ford owners knew that on a cold morning, they could start their T more readily by pouring hot water on the manifold or by applying a blow torch to it. The Simon Primer was guaranteed to heat up the entire manifold by electricity in ten seconds. The Hot Spot Primer in 1922 consisted of a shallow bowl attached under one wing of the manifold. The driver dipped a metal-covered wick in gasoline or alcohol and, placing it in the pan, allowed it to burn for a minute or so, thus heating up the manifold for "easy starting in any temperature." One of the most interesting of these devices was a fire trap built into an extraordinary manifold. It provided a little stove into which the driver could stuff rags or paper, touch a match to them, then close the door and let the burning flotsam heat up the manifold with safety.

If the ignition system of the Model T went dead, or at least left something to be desired in the way of en-

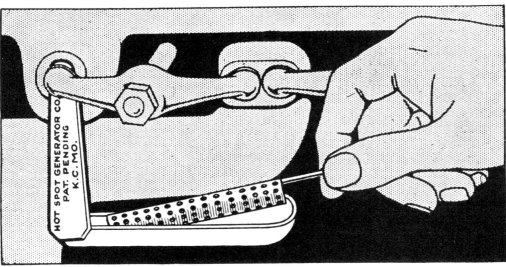

One dollar in the early twenties bought you this "Hot Spot Generator" which warmed up the intake manifold on cold mornings, assuring prompt starting of your Model T.

gine performance, the accessory manufacturers filled in the gaps with supposedly non-fouling spark plugs and different timers—or commutators, as they were frequently called, a word which has obviously fallen by the wayside. Many types of magnetos were offered. One of the most popular ignition systems before the 1920s was the Atwater Kent system, which made its inventor and namesake a fortune.

Most roads before 1920 were of dirt or sharp rocks or merely trails with high centers, and the Model T crankcase was especially vulnerable to rough roads. A broken crankcase and the smell of dry, burning metal often distressed the driver when he was nowhere close to a garage. Gemco of Milwaukee sold a special crankcase support for $2.50, on which the driver could "save himself $20." This saving was figured at $22.50 for a new crankcase and $7.50 for labor. Gemco's ads insisted that every venturesome tourist needed their crankcase support, and for a time it was a common assumption.

To serve the happy vagabond who left town in his flivver, the accessory makers built tire carriers and luggage racks that attached to the running boards, to the rear or top of the car, or between the front fender and the hood. Parking lights and rear-wheel grease retainers were also offered, along with bumpers, for country or city driving.

With some mechanical ingenuity or the services of a local mechanic, the T owner might build into his stock model features that gave it amazing added performance, not to mention looks. The T was adaptable to many kinds of motoring tastes. It was this appeal to the tinkerer instinct, as much as economy and performance, that established Ford's T as The Car on the American country road up until the late twenties. And if Henry Ford offered few accessories in the initial years of the T, he did furnish a complete set of tools—far more than the modern car owner gets—and the driver knew how to use them!

One of the unusual accessories for the Ford was a front-wheel-axle-and-differential assembly, to make a

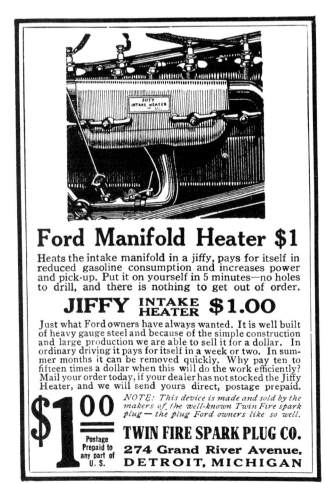

A 1919 ad offering a Model T manifold heater which used exhaust heat to heat the intake manifold "in a jiffy."

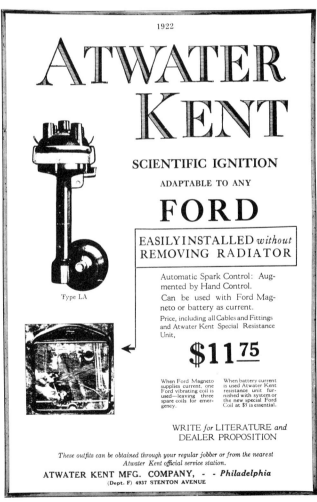

A 1922 ad for the Atwater Kent "scientific ignition" system. AK was to become more prominent in radio manufacture, for which he is remembered today; his battery sets are collector's items.

A 1922 ad for luggage carriers. Note the practical way it could be folded out of the way when not in use.

Part of a 1921 ad selling a Shurnuff Grease Retainer "absolutely guaranteed" to stop rear-end grease leaks with their patented retainer, all for ninety cents. Another ad suggesting the reader see his Ford dealer for the item.

four-wheel-drive Model T. For the park gardener, road repairman or the sand and gravel dealer, there were special dump truck bodies for half-ton or larger truck frames. Iron shops offered to convert your T frame into the right kind of truck chassis and body for your particular needs. They welded extensions onto the frame to lengthen the wheelbase and added extra-heavy springs to carry the load. Thus emerged, side by side with the stock car a type of vehicle called the "truck," a development to which the Model T made an important contribution.

The village of Highland Park, Michigan, a Detroit suburb of 30,000, purchased a Model T Runabout and in 1916 converted it into an excellent piece of fire-fighting equipment, carrying a chemical tank, a 30 gallon fire extinguisher and 150 feet of ¾ in. hose. Other small cities throughout the country rigged up similar vehicles on the theory that horses were impractical when twenty seconds at the beginning of a fire were—and still are—worth twenty minutes later on.

A 1922 ad for a Model T antitheft steering wheel lock. It was made operable in conjunction with the steering wheel, which itself was made impossible to remove.

"Oilomatik" Engine Lubricators

Proper lubrication of an engine is essential if one does not want engine failure. The primitive oiling system of the Model T guaranteed the appearance of aftermarket oiling systems promising no-trouble results.

WANTED

Salesmen—
Distributors—
State Managers

TO SELL

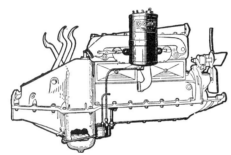

What Does OILOMATIK Do?

It maintains a constant oil level in the crank case of a Ford—

And in doing so saves 25 to 50 per cent in oil consumption, and absolutely eliminates the possible chance of running your FORD without the proper amount of lubrication, as it automatically **blows your horn** when low level is reached.

Our men now making from $5000 to $10,000 a year—send us the attached coupon **today** and get in on our

10-DAY FREE TRIAL

OILOMATIK SALES CO.
Dept. 2, 341 East Ohio St., CHICAGO, ILL.

Gentlemen: At no obligation to me, please send full particulars of your 10-day free trial proposition to

☐ **Salesman** ☐ **Distributor** ☐ **State Manager**

(Check the one you are interested in.)

The Model T owner occasionally had trouble with car thieves and "borrowers" who just wanted to see how the thing drove. Dozens of different kinds of locks were marketed that could be mounted on the steering wheel. Others locked the front wheel to the axle or radius rod. One type set the front spindle so that the front wheel would not turn. There were ignition locks and one odd type made of hinged iron that encircled the rim and tire. A sharp spike protruded. If a thief tried to drive away, the spike would lift the wheel off the ground as it revolved.

For cold weather, there appeared a variety of hood and radiator covers to keep Lizzie warm. These were used by so many drivers that by 1927, they were practically standard equipment on the Model T. Usually made of leather or heavy canvas, they sold for $1.95 to $3.50 and were supposed to be indispensable to the driver who wanted heat control for his engine.

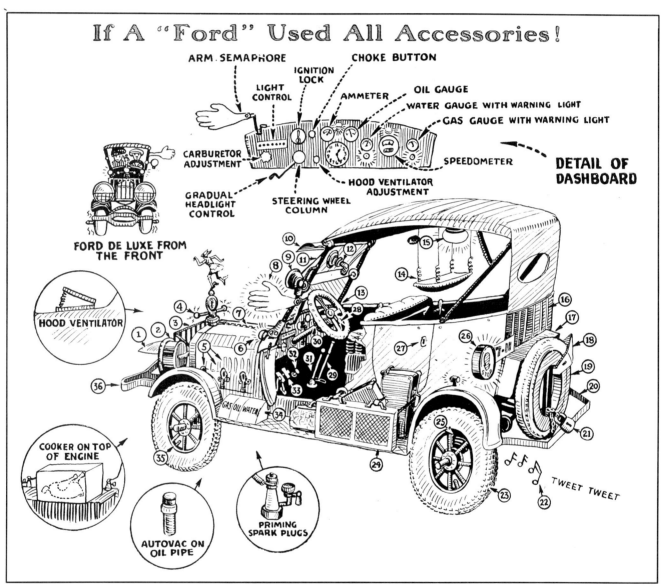

A cartoon from a 1925 issue of Science and Invention, satirizing the great number of "accessories" available for the Model T. Items are identified as follows: 1. visor for headlights; 2. barrel headlights; 3. radiator shield; 4. motormeter, electrically lighted, surmounted by figure of Mercury; 5. spring hood clamps; 6. hood lights; 7. special carburetor; 8. arm semaphore; 9. combination spot and trouble light with mirror back; 10. sun visor; 11. slanted windshield; 12. spotlight, trained from behind windshield; 13. electrically heated steering wheel; 14. baby carrier; 15. domelight in tonneau; 16. brass strips to protect paint; 17. trunk; 18. spike theft preventer; 19. spare tire carrier; 20. rear bumper attached to mudguards; 21. spare tire lock; 22. exhaust whistle; 23. oversize tires; 24. luggage carrier; 25. shock absorbers; 26. Wright stop signal; 27. door locks; 28. watch on steering wheel; 29. brake; 30. steering column lock; 31. gearshift lever; 32. accelerator; 33. non-slip pedals; 34. emergency gas, water and oil; 35. visible tire gauge; 36. front bumper.

Heaters also for drivers and passengers appeared on the market in large numbers. Some were simply pieces of sheet metal that bolted over the exhaust manifold so that the heat from the manifold filtered into the body. Some of the best car heaters I ever enjoyed were used on the Model T and they sold for as little as $1.75, installed! There was not much control—only a sliding metal door—but lots of heat.

"Standardized equipment" have almost become bywords in mass automobile design and production. Though some 5,000 gadgets and devices were produced during the nineteen-year course of the T's life, relatively few have survived. Yet inventors, home garage mechanics, tinkerers and bright young factory men had put their ingenuity to good use. The automobile companies and the American public shared in the real benefits when, years later, these or similar accessories became standard equipment on production models.

Even though Ford never officially recognized any of the early independently produced accessories, he ultimately began to make his own accessories for the Model T. Towards the end of the Model T's life, the company actually began selling Ford Approved items; the dealers began selling them, at any rate. But it was all water over the dam.

In the twenties, Henry Ford's son Edsel became president of the company, although Henry Ford still ruled with an iron hand. Edsel, a brilliant man, could do little with his father, but he did see the handwriting on the wall—that the famous old Model T was beginning to sputter and run out of popularity. Other makes had progressed with good strides, but Mr. Ford wanted still to force the T on the American motorist. Edsel, at last, convinced his father that the T would have to give way to a more modern car, with a three-speed transmission and four-wheel brakes.

So Henry, almost alone, set out to design his Model A to replace his beloved Model T. The change-over was a long, drawn-out, painful and dramatic process. As brilliant as Ford was, he took so long to make the conversion that many Ford dealers, who for years had been geared for volume selling, nearly went broke while waiting for the new Ford Model A to appear in 1928.

No automobile can ever take the place in the hearts of so many motorists that the Model T occupied for the nineteen years it was manufactured.

There can never be another Henry Ford or another Model T. Millions regretted the passing of both, and, in the generations to come, the legend of Henry Ford and his famous Tin Lizzie will never die.

Chapter 3

The Art of Driving a Model T

Murray Fahnestock

The idea that "anyone can drive a Model T Ford"
wrecked more Model T reputations than all else
its competitors could throw against it

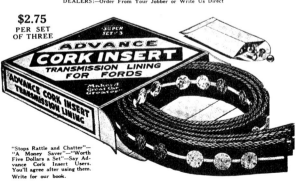
A 1922 ad for a replacement for Ford transmission linings. The use of cork implanted in the lining was supposed to produce superior results.

There is a difference between driving a Model T and driving a conventional car which many owners of these antique cars never seemed to learn. For instance:

How do you tramp on the three foot pedals?

How do you grasp the handle of the parking brake?

How do you shake hands with the starting crank?

Aside from early tires, the most troublesome parts of the Model T Fords were the transmission band linings which not only engaged the low and reverse gears, but also, and most importantly, functioned as brakes. Many car owners failed to understand that when these band linings "chattered," as they so often did, they were trying to tell the "secret" of the Model T Ford that. . . .

"Deep within the transmission hide. . . .
Oil-cooled brakes on their inward side."

Hard and soft linings of all kinds were tried for the transmission bands of Model T Fords. The hard linings were harsh in action and "chattered" badly, and the soft cotton linings were smooth in action and gave long wear—if (and it was a big "if") they were not charred by heat!

Cotton is a poor conductor of heat from the "inside surface" in contact with the drum (where the heat is created) to the steel band on the outside of the lining. Consequently, the heat builds up and chars the vital surface of the lining, if one of these linings is kept steadily against a drum.

The big secret is to use the big supply of oil in the lower part of the transmission to cool the vital, inside surface of the cotton band linings. Moving the foot from the reverse pedal to the brake pedal, or momentarily releasing the braking pedal, every two or three seconds, allows the oil to reach the vital, inside surface of the linings and produce the effect of "oil-cooled"

Easy On and Off Demountables

A comical drawing, satirizing the frequent need for the Model T driver to get to the spark lever and advance the spark "before she dies!"

A 1924 ad for a safety cranking device. It is difficult today to comprehend why Ford could have made five million Model Ts without starters. Although several makes adopted starters in 1912, Ford waited until 1919 and then offered starters as options only.

brakes. One early Model T transcontinental tourist told us that he had driven almost from coast to coast by using this procedure carefully. If the procedure is not used, the transmission linings could easily burn out on one long, steep hill.

Before attempting to start the engine, always be sure to apply the parking brake securely. Grasp the handle with the four fingers around the handle (with the little finger on top) and the thumb pressed against the latch (on the back side of the handle) to avoid the noise of the ratchet, until the brake is firmly engaged,

then release the latch. Since the parking brake handle also disengages the high-speed clutch, firm application of the brake handle is necessary to keep the car from running over the driver when the engine is started. Never use this parking brake for anything but emergencies or for parking, since the brake drums on the rear wheels are small to keep the rear axle light, and the unlined brake shoes wear out quickly.

Many an arm has been fractured by the improper use of the starting crank. The secret is to use the left hand and to pull up with the thumb on the same side of the handle as the fingers. Then if a backfire occurs (as has been known to happen), the reverse action of the crank jerks the handle out of the driver's hand and throws the hand away from the starting crank. A strong pull upward on the starting crank also tends to utilize the momentum of the flywheel to continue the proper rotation of the crankshaft, in spite of a minor tendency to backfire. Never push down on the starting crank and get your elbow in a straight line from handle to shoulder, for if a backfire occurs then something has to give—and it won't be the starting crank!

Chapter 4

Outwitting the Model T

Les Henry

No man ever was complete master of the Tin Lizzie

Simple in the extreme and lacking in many comforts, the Ford Model T seemed always to run despite adversity. But she ran her best for the man with a wrench, an understanding heart and an imagination. Such was old Sam in our town, and his knowledge of Model T lore and his methods of meeting her foibles gave him a professional status along with Doc and the Judge.

In balmy weather, Tin Lizzie (the Model T, of course) was always ready to go places; her planetary transmission was limber and her "hot shot" dry battery was strong. In fact, she would often start right up "on compression" the instant her switch was turned on, provided that she had a charge of gas in the cylinder and her spark lever was set on the fourth notch.

Sam used to show her off this way down in the village; he'd pull up on the crank a few times to compres-

sion, set the spark on the third notch, turn on the switch—and leave her! Returning with some cronies, Sam would nonchalantly step up to Tin Lizzie and give her front tire a swift kick. This really shook Miss Model T to her frame; the vibration jiggled the spark lever down to the fourth notch and sent the hot spark buzzing down to start her engine with a mighty roar!

There were all kinds of driving techniques. Doc's wife knew she always had time to read the letters on the three pedals and to press the one marked "C" (for clutch) to start off, but she didn't always have time to look for the pedal marked "B" (for brake). So she would stomp down on both pedals (whichever happened to be under her feet at the time!) to stop both car and engine at the same time!

A 1922 ad for a divided gasoline tank, to assure "3 to 5 miles" of travel after regular tank runs dry.

A 1924 ad for a power takeoff via the regular crank connection. Most such power takeoffs utilized a rear power takeoff as mentioned in the article.

Now, Sam used to pump a player piano, so it was the easiest thing in the world for him to transfer his footwork to Miss Lizzie's brake and reverse pedals. That was real technique! It not only distributed wear evenly between the two bands but on the long downhill to the village, it allowed the oil to replenish itself between the bands and the drums often enough so that the cotton linings would not "burn."

Sam backed his Tin Lizzie up that hill only once, when he was low on gas and the incline raised her carburetor higher than the level in her under-seat gravity-fed gas tank. After that, he carried a spare tank cap fitted with an inner-tube valve stem so that he could pressurize the gas tank with his air pump.

Starting the Model T in winter was often a serious chore, calling for brawn with brains. The planetary transmission ran in a bath of engine oil which caused a terrific drag between the many moving parts when cold. It was all a strong man could do just to turn the hand crank, let alone spin it to start. Sam was far from strong, so on mildly chilly nights he wouldn't use the hand brake but would put Miss Lizzie in high gear, to

Transmission Cure-Alls 1920–1924

The planetary gear system was the most talked-about feature of the Model T. Despite its limitations, it did have one advantage over the progressive-type transmission used by others—there never was any clashing of gears, so typical of all early non-synchromesh transmissions. The tendency of such cars equipped with an epicyclic transmission to creep is only reminiscent of today's automatics in which one has to keep a foot on the brake to prevent similar creeping.

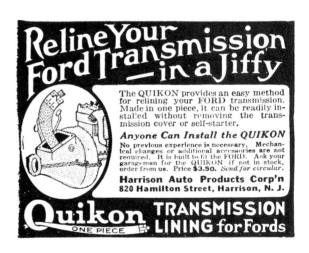
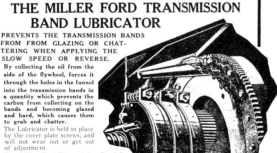

keep the oil squeezed out of the multiple disc clutch. Next a.m., he'd apply the hand brake to release the oilless clutch and she'd crank over like nothing!

Sam used to say that he started his Lizzie with a two-by-four. And he did, too—on really cold days! He'd tilt a fifteen-inch stud against the rear axle near a wheel; then, with both hands behind his back, he'd lift up the wheel about an inch until the two-by-four would tip forward and stand under the axle. Best darned jack you ever saw—and was great for changing tires too!

Well, after Sam had Tin Lizzie standing with one wheel in the air, and the others well chocked, he'd put her in high gear and wind her up with the crank. Having no clutch drag, the transmission and jacked-up rear wheel would act as flywheels and really keep her engine spinning until she started.

Draining Model T on cold nights, then pouring hot oil in the engine and hot water in the radiator were starting practices employed only by unplanetary persons lacking in ingenuity.

One of the major appliances Sam attached to his Lizzie was a large pressed steel pulley bolted to a rear wheel which, when jacked up, provided a ready source for sawing wood and filling the silo. But such intermittent loading and idling service got the engine to pump-

ing oil and fouling the spark plugs. Sam solved this problem by screwing half-inch pipe elbows into the cylinder head and then putting the spark plugs into the side of the elbow, out of the way of the oil.

Since tires were the most expensive items attached to a Model T, owners sought to get the most out of them, naturally. As the tires wore thin, liners professionally cut from other old tires were inserted, and blowout patches were carried in the sub-cushion regions of the car. When Sam mounted a new tire he would protect it for a while by cutting up old tires in segments and wiring them over the new tire like overshoes. And to repair a puncture, he'd never bother to jack up Tin Lizzie but would just pry up one edge of the clincher tire from the rim, pull out enough of the inner tube to apply a patch, then poke the tube back in and pump it up—to fifty pounds.

Sam always wore a bolt with suspenders—not because he was cautious, but because he never knew when he might have to cut up the belt and replace a broken fan belt or cushion a burned-out connection rod bearing!

No man ever was complete master of a Model T but, true to her gender, Miss Tin Lizzie was a willing servant to him who gave her proper care.

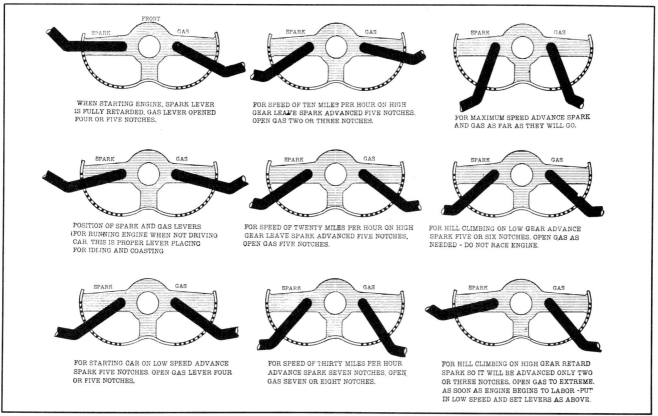

Chart showing positions of spark-throttle levers on steering post quadrants for various conditions of car operation. These are average positions and may have varied slightly on Fords, depending on the year.

Chapter 5

Driving and Maintaining Ford Cars

Victor W. Pagé

Words of wisdom from one of the pioneering
sages of the horseless carriage

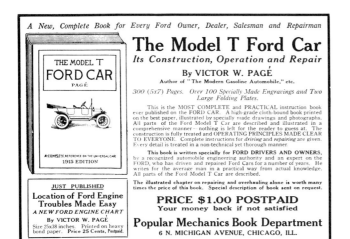

Victor W. Page's car guides were popular and numerous.

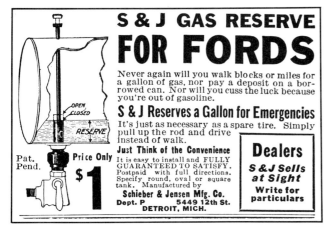

A 1923 ad for an auxiliary gas tank. Simply "pull up on the rod" and, presto, enough gas so you "drive instead of walk." No mention is made if this tank is larger than the regular Model T tank or if the same-sized tank is just divided into two parts.

Steps before starting the engine

Before attempting to start the motor, there are a number of preliminary precautions to be taken in order to make sure that the car is ready for the road. The gasoline container of the Ford automobile has a capacity of ten gallons, and this should be filled practically to the top. In order to determine the amount of fuel available, a measuring stick may be introduced into the top filler opening to gauge the supply of liquid in the container.

As gasoline vapor is explosive, it is well to make sure that there are no naked flames within several feet of the tank when it is being filled or the contents of the tank checked. When filling the tank at night, be sure that all the side lights are extinguished before any fuel is poured. The small vent holes in the fuel tank cap should always be free, as if they are plugged up, it will prevent the gasoline from flowing into the carburetor, because of the suction created.

Before starting out, always make sure that the proper supply of medium body, high grade gas engine cylinder oil is poured into the crank case through the breather pipe at the front of the engine. This opening is covered by a brass cap which may be easily withdrawn as it is held in place only by frictional contact. In the back of the lower part of the flywheel casing, which is also the reservoir that holds the oil, are found two petcocks. Pour in the oil slowly until it runs out the upper petcock. Have a can so that the oil running out will be saved. Leave this petcock open until the oil stops running, then close it.

After the car has been used long enough for the engine to become thoroughly free and easy running, the best results will be obtained by carrying the oil at a level about midway between the two petcocks. If the lower petcock is opened and no oil comes out, a proper supply should be immediately placed in the crank case.

Having made sure that there is a proper supply of fuel and oil, the next step is to insure that the cooling supply is adequate. Remove the cap at the top of the radiator and fill with clean water. The Ford cooling system has a capacity of slightly more than three gallons of water. Never run the engine unless the radiator is filled. Water should be poured in until it starts to run out the overflow pipe.

How to start the Ford motor

The essential precautions enumerated, having been taken, the first step in starting the motor is to look at the steering wheel and notice the position of the spark and throttle control levers. The right hand lever is called a "throttle" as it controls the amount of gaseous mixture drawn into the motor. When the power plant is in operation the nearer the operator that this lever is, the faster the engine will turn and the greater the power output.

The left hand lever controls the spark which should be in retarded position or at its extreme position, away from the operator, when starting the motor. It is possible in many cases to advance this lever three or four notches towards the operator without any injury during cranking. The throttle lever should be placed about four or five notches down to secure easy starting. The reason it is desired not to advance the spark lever too far is that the engine may kick back.

A kick back can result in a sprained or even in a broken arm, so the proper procedure should always be used; that is, always pull *up* on the crank, never push *down*! Any kick back then will throw the crank out and away from the operator safely.

Before cranking, one should make sure that the emergency brake lever is pulled back as far as it will go. When in this position, the clutch is out and the hub

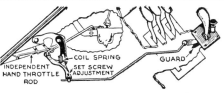
Several firms offered a means of converting the manual throttle lever to foot operation. This is a 1922 ad.

Another 1922 ad offering a safety device to prevent accidents resulting from cranking Model Ts. No explanation is given on how the device allowed the motor to "reverse"—only possible on two-cycle engines. Even more astonishing is the statement that in 1921, seventy percent of Fords were sold without starters.

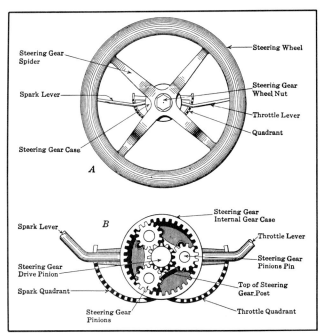

Steering Gear Spider

Spark Lever

Steering Gear Case

A

Steering Wheel

Steering Gear Wheel Nut

Throttle Lever

Quadrant

Spark Lever

Steering Gear Drive Pinion

Spark Quadrant

Steering Gear Pinions

B

Steering Gear Internal Gear Case

Throttle Lever

Steering Gear Pinions Pin

Top of Steering Gear Post

Throttle Quadrant

Drawing indicating position of spark and throttle levers as well as quadrants.

brakes are engaged, which prevents the car from moving. After inserting the switch key in the switch on the coil box, throw the switch lever as far to the left as it will go, toward the point marked "magneto." If batteries are used as an auxiliary it may be possible to start the engine easier on the battery current, though a very easy start may be secured on the magneto, provided the coil vibrators are properly adjusted.

The next step is to crank the engine by lifting on the crank. Take hold of the handle and push the crank in until you feel the ratchet engage with the pin passing through the crank shaft. Then pull the handle up with a quick swing.

If the car has been standing for some time, it is advisable to prime the carburetor by pulling on the small wire on the lower left corner of the radiator, while giving the engine two or three quarter turns with the handle. In this case, the crank should be grasped by the

The Weeks Company was one of the big advertisers of the mid twenties with such ads as this, promising more power and better fuel economy—all accomplished with the Weeks' positive automatic primer. Emphasis, however, is on easy starting in cold weather, a reputed Model T weakness.

right hand but care should be taken to only pull *up* against compression. In cold weather, gasoline does not evaporate rapidly so it is somewhat more difficult to start an engine under these conditions.

The method recommended by the Ford Motor Company for starting the engine when cold is to turn the carburetor dash adjustment one quarter turn to the left to allow a richer mixture of gasoline to be drawn into the cylinders, then to hold out the priming rod which projects through the radiator, while the crank is whirled vigorously. Another method is as follows: Before throwing on the magneto switch, close the throttle lever, hold out the priming rod while you give the crank several quick turns, then let go of the priming rod, place the spark lever in the third or fourth notch position, advance the throttle several notches, throw on the switch and crank briskly.

After starting the motor, it is advisable to advance the spark half way down the quadrant and to let the motor run until thoroughly warmed up. If one starts out with a cold motor, it is likely not to have much power and it will be easy to "stall" it. It is said that the advantage of turning on the switch last after priming is that there is plenty of gas in the cylinders to keep the motor running. After the motor is warmed up, the carburetor adjustment should be turned back to the normal running position.

If, for any reason, the engine is warm and does not start readily, it is probably because the engine has been flooded with an over rich mixture of gas. The remedy for this is to turn the carburetor adjusting needle down by screwing the needle valve on the dash to the right until the needle seats in the carburetor. Crank the engine briskly to exhaust the rich gas, then throw on the switch and start the engine. As soon as the cylinders fire, turn the needle back to the normal running position.

If the engine still fails to start, the following defective conditions may be responsible: Water in the gasoline; water or hardened oil in commutator; coil vibrators out of adjustment; gas mixture too thin; gas mixture too rich; magneto contact point in transmission cover raised because of foreign matter or short circuiting by a piece of wire from brake lining; gasoline supply shut off; water frozen in gasoline tank sediment bulb; poor contact at coil switch; loose magneto wire leading to coil; loose timer wires; engine too cold to properly vaporize gas (only in zero weather).

Should the engine start, run for a time and suddenly stop, one should make sure that there is plenty of fuel. The trouble may be a flooded carburetor; dirt in carburetor or feed pipe; magneto loose wire at either terminal; magneto collecting point obstructed; engine overheated on account of insufficient oil or water supply.

If the engine lacks power and runs irregularly, called "skipping" at low speed, it may be due to: Imperfect gas mixture; dirty spark plugs; poorly adjusted coil vibrators; poor compression; air leak through intake manifold; weak exhaust valve springs, too little clearance between valve stem and push rod; spark plug points too close together.

If the engine misfires at high speed, it may result from imperfect contact in the interior of the commutator; too much air gap between the spark plug points; imperfect gas mixture or poorly adjusted vibrators. When an engine overheats, the most common condition is running with too rich a gas mixture and a retarded spark. Other troubles are: Insufficient lubricating oil; not enough water in the radiator; fan belt slipping; poor water circulation, owing to sediment in radiator tubes; or a carbon deposit in the combustion chambers. These deposits may be also present on the piston heads and will result in loss of power as well as produce a knocking sound. A more pronounced knocking sound will generally be due to a loose connecting rod or a worn crank shaft bearing or running with the spark advanced too far and is always a sign of a badly overheated engine.

Controlling the Ford car

The Ford car is one of the most popular of moderate-priced cars and over 600,000 of the Model T are now on the road. The control system of this car is extremely simple and yet it is different from that of any other automobile. The gearset is a planetary type which gives two forward speeds and one reverse. It is the method of obtaining the various speed ratios that is distinctive.

Three pedals and a hand lever are provided on the left side of the car. The pedal on the extreme left controls both the high and low-speed clutches, the center pedal is for reverse and the right pedal is the brake.

The hand lever engages the high speed or direct drive clutch when thrown forward and when pulled back, it actuates the emergency brake, which cannot be applied without releasing the direct drive clutch. The lever may be set in neutral position and the clutch will be released without applying the brake when it is approximately vertical. When the high speed is in and the hand lever is thrown full forward, the high speed clutch may be released by a light pressure on the clutch (left hand) pedal. A further movement of this pedal will bring in low gear. Thus one pedal controls both low and high gear, with the clutch being released in exactly the same manner as that of a sliding gear arrangement on other cars, when it is desired to slow up, such as for turning a corner, ascending a hill or passing another vehicle.

Before starting the car, the hand lever must be in a vertical position, thus releasing the clutch and applying the emergency brake. To start the car, after the engine has been started, the foot is placed on the clutch pedal to keep it in neutral position, while the hand lever is thrown as far forward as it will go. The engine is then accelerated and the clutch pedal is pushed forward until the slow speed band tightens around the drum of the transmission, and the car gathers headway on the lower ratio. After it has attained a certain momentum, the clutch pedal is allowed to drop back gradually into the high speed position. The foot may then be removed until such time that the clutch must be disconnected. Before applying the brake, which is done by pressing the right foot on the brake pedal, the clutch pedal should be put in neutral with the left foot.

To reverse the car, with the car at a stand-still, the engine is kept running while the clutch is disengaged with the hand lever, which is placed in neutral position but not pulled back far enough to apply the emergency brake. The reverse pedal is then pushed forward with the left foot, leaving the right one free to use on the brake pedal if necessary.

To stop the car, the throttle is closed so the engine will not race; the high speed clutch is released by pressing it forward into neutral position and applying the foot brake slowly but firmly, until the forward motion of the car is arrested. It is imperative that the foot brake be retained on the clutch pedal until the hand brake is pulled back to its neutral position. The placing of the spark and throttle levers are both pulled back to accelerate the motor and pushed forward to slow it down.

General driving instructions

The gear shift lever should always be placed in neutral when the car is stopped, whether it is left alone or attended. The clutch should always be applied gradually and as slowly as possible. Never allow the engine to race when changing speeds. When changing down from high to low speed, allow the car to slow down until its speed is about the same as that which will be produced by the lower gear ratio desired before the clutch is engaged to produce the lower speed.

Always drive slowly and cautiously until you are thoroughly familiar with the control mechanism and the methods of stopping the car. When driving up grades in high, if the motor shows any tendency to labor, shift back into the low gear. One should never attempt to drive Ford cars at high speed unless the tire casings are in perfect condition and the road surfaces good. Brakes should be carefully applied, especially if the road surfaces are wet. Never stop in mud, clay, sand, snow or slush if it can be avoided. Whenever

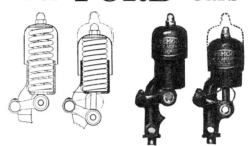

road conditions are unfavorable, the driving wheels should be fitted with tire chains.

All motorists should familiarize themselves as much as possible with the mechanism of their car and should feel competent enough to make the ordinary adjustments and minor repairs before any long trips are attempted. The manufacturer's instructions should be followed as closely as possible because intelligent care means long life and reliable service.

Suggestions for oiling

One of the most important points to be observed in connection with gasoline automobile operation is that all parts be oiled regularly. It is not enough to apply lubricant indiscriminately to the various chassis parts. It must be done systematically and logically to secure the best results and ensure economical use of lubricants. The most important parts are the power plant and the transmission and the engine is but one part of the car that must be properly oiled at all times to obtain satisfactory results.

Some of the running-gear parts are relatively unimportant, others demand regular inspection and oiling. Some of the points are governed by special instructions, these being the transmission case, timer and rear axle. Use only the best medium body cylinder oil in the Ford motor. The writer has obtained excellent results by putting in a quart of lubricant to every five gallons of gasoline. The oil was introduced through the breather pipe every time that amount of gas was placed in the tank.

Neither the transmission case nor the differential case on the rear axle should be filled with heavy "dope" widely sold which may contain fiber or cork particles to make for more silent operation. If any gears are noisy, it is either because they are worn out or out of adjustment and the use of nostrums and freak lubricants will not improve their use or silence noisy gears. The rear axle differential housing should be filled with as light mineral grease as it is possible to get, those having the consistency of Vaseline and containing graphite being most desirable. Light oils should not be used in the rear axle housing because they will tend to leak out over the brakes and have not sufficient body to cushion the gear teeth.

The only other point on the chart which needs explanation is lubrication of the timer interior. This should be oiled as it is a roller contact form and a few drops of magneto or 3-in-1 oil should be applied to the roll and contact segments once a week. The timer case should be removed and all old, dirty oil washed out with gasoline before fresh lubricant is applied. Never use graphite or any heavy oil in a timer case because these will not only interfere with regular ignition by short circuiting the current, but they will also clog up the timer and prevent the roller establishing proper contact with the segments.

After the car is oiled, it is well to go over all the exposed joints with a piece of cloth to remove the ac-

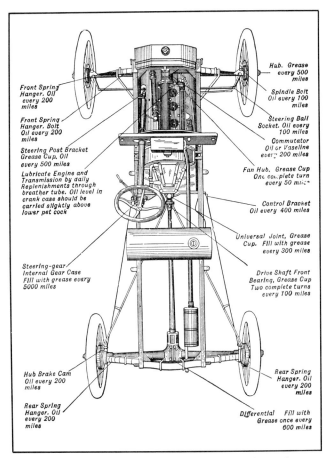

Top view of Model T chassis showing lubrication points.

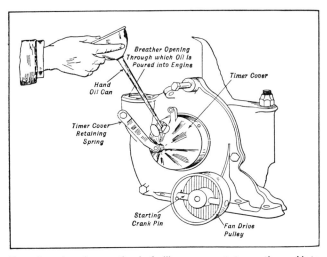

Drawing showing method of oiling commutator or timer. Note breather opening behind the timer through which crankcase oil was poured.

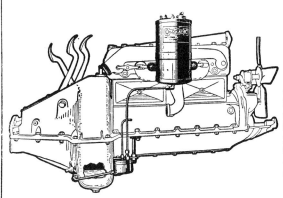
A 1921 ad for an automatic oiling system for the Model T Ford. This is perhaps the most important item that the car should have possessed. It should at least have been offered as an option.

cumulation of surplus oil on the outside of the parts. The simplicity of the Ford makes for easy lubrication as the entire mechanism can be thoroughly oiled in less than five minutes. The places needing lubrication, itemized under the heads of mileage covered, follow:

Lubricate after 200 miles' driving

Lubricant	Number	Name of parts
Oil	2	Front axle, steering knuckle pivots or spindle bolts
Oil	2	Front spring shackles and bolts
Oil	2	Yokes of tie rod
Oil	1	Steering ball socket
Oil	1	Commutator or timer
Oil	2	Rear hub brake cams
Oil	2	Rear spring shackles and bolts
Turn grease cup	1	Fan hub

Lubricate after 500 miles' driving

Turn grease cup	1	Steering post bracket
Turn grease cup	1	Universal joint of shaft
Turn grease cup	1	Driving shaft front bearing
Grease	2	Front wheel hubs

Lubricate after 1,000 miles' driving

Grease	1	Differential housing

Lubricate after 2,000 miles' driving

Oil	1	Control bracket

Lubricate after 5,000 miles' driving

Grease	1	Steering gear internal gear case

Lubricate daily

Oil	1	Motor

Lubricate occasionally

Oil	1	Fan belt shaft
Oil	1	Fan belt pulley
Oil	1	Crank handle bearing
Oil	4	Yokes of brake rods

In referring to the oiling process, this means using a sufficient quantity to lubricate the bearing parts thoroughly and turning the grease cups means checking to see that they are full. Greasing means packing the bearing or housing until it is full. When full, screw down each grease cup three times. This will ensure an ample supply of lubricant reaching the bearing. Care should be taken to wipe the cups clean before filling to prevent dirt from reaching the bearings and the oilers should be cleaned similarly.

The best attention can be given at the end of the day's or night's driving, which will require very little time. The engine should be wiped clean while it is warm. The fourth time the oil cups are turned, they can be left for the stated mileage interval. With the radiator and engine oil checked out, the driver can be sure that he can drive to the next stated interval without fear of trouble.

In the process of oiling everything, the driver will be able to note whether or not there is wear on any of the moving parts, and one will find that there is usually need of tightening nuts and screws that have loosened. Needless to say, steps should be taken to remedy any such conditions.

Winter care of automobiles

While motoring throughout the entire year is not unusual, many owners of cars, especially in those portions of the country where the winter climate is exceptionally severe, put up their cars for the winter period. If the car is kept in service, the most important thing to do is to provide some good anti-freeze compound to prevent the water in the radiator and cylinders from congealing. There is some difference of opinion regarding the best solution to use to prevent cracked water jackets and burst radiators.

Before we attempt to answer the questions often asked regarding the best anti-freeze compound, it will be well to consider the requirements of such compounds. To begin with, it should have no deleterious effects on the metals or rubber used in the circulating system. It must be easily dissolved or combined with water, should be reasonably cheap, and not subject to waste by evaporation. The boiling point should be higher than water to prevent boiling away of the solution at comparatively low temperature.

Solutions of calcium chloride have been very popular with motorists, and the writer will first discuss the use of this substance. The freezing point of the solution depends upon the proportion of the salt to the water. An important factor to consider is that if the parts of the circulation system are composed of different metals, there is liable to be a certain electrolytic action between the salt and the dissimilar metals at the points of juncture, a certain corrosion taking place, and the intensity of this corrosive effect is dependent upon the strength of the solution.

As calcium chloride is derived from hydrochloric acid, which has a very strong effect on metals, a certain undesired corrosive effect may take place. In using calcium chloride when compounding an anti-freeze solution, care must be taken that commercially-pure salt is employed, as the cruder grades will liberate a larger percentage of free acid. The mistake should not be

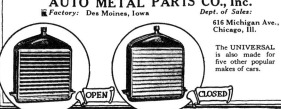

A 1924 ad for a radiator shutter to control Model T engine temperature in winter, also said to "add to the appearance of your car summer or winter."

Keeps You Snug and Warm

Another device for adding to winter driving comfort, the 1922 Kingston heater. When one notices the low price of such a desirable feature, one wonders why the factory at least didn't offer such an optional feature.

made of using chloride of lime, which has much the same appearance, but the corrosive action of which is very great.

It is well to test a solution of calcium chloride for acid before placing it in the radiator. A piece of blue litmus paper may be obtained at any drug store and immersed in the solution. If the paper turns red, it is a sign of acid being present. Acid may be neutralized by the addition of a small quantity of slacked lime. The solutions may be made in these proportions:

Two pounds of salt to a gallon of water will freeze at eighteen degrees Fahrenheit.

Three pounds of salt to a gallon of water will freeze at one and five-tenths degrees Fahrenheit.

Four pounds of salt to the gallon will freeze at seventeen degrees Fahrenheit below zero.

Five pounds of salt to the gallon will freeze at thirty-nine degrees Fahrenheit below zero.

It must be remembered that the more salt to the solution, the greater the electrolytic effect and the greater the liability of the deposit of salt crystals which may obstruct the free flow of the liquid.

Glycerine is usually considered quite favorably, but it has disadvantages. It often contains free acid, though the action on metals will be imperceptible in average solutions. While it does not attack metal piping to any extent, it is sure destruction to rubber hose and should not be used in a car in which part of the circulation system piping is rubber. Glycerine is expensive and it is liable to decompose under the influence of heat and proportions added to the water must be higher than for other substances.

Denatured alcohol is without doubt the best substance to use as it does not have any destructive action on the metals or rubber hose, will not form deposits of foreign matter, and has no electrolytic effect. A solution of sixty per cent water and forty per cent alcohol will stand twenty-five degrees below zero without freezing. The chief disadvantage to its use is that it evaporates more rapidly than water and the solution is liable to become too light as alcohol evaporates. The percentages required are as follows:

Water, ninety-five percent; alcohol, 5 percent; freezes at twenty-five degrees Fahrenheit.

Water, eighty-five percent; alcohol, fifteen percent; freezes at eleven degrees Fahrenheit.

Water, eighty percent; alcohol, twenty percent; freezes at five degrees Fahrenheit.

Water, seventy percent; alcohol, thirty percent; freezes at nine degrees Fahrenheit below zero.

Water, sixty-five percent; alcohol, thirty-five percent; freezes at sixteen degrees Fahrenheit below zero.

Various mixtures have been tried of alcohol, glycerine and water, and good results obtained. The addition of glycerine to a water-alcohol solution reduces the liability of evaporation to a large extent, and when glycerine is used in such proportions it is not liable to damage the rubber hose. The proportions recommended are a solution of half glycerine and half alcohol to water. The glycerine in such a solution will remain practically the same, not subject to evaporation, and water and alcohol must be supplied if the amount of solution in the radiator is not enough.

The freezing temperatures of such solutions of varying proportions are as follows:

Water, eighty-five percent; alcohol and glycerine, fifteen percent; freezes at twenty degrees Fahrenheit.

Water, seventy-five percent; alcohol and glycerine, twenty-five percent; freezes at eight degrees Fahrenheit.

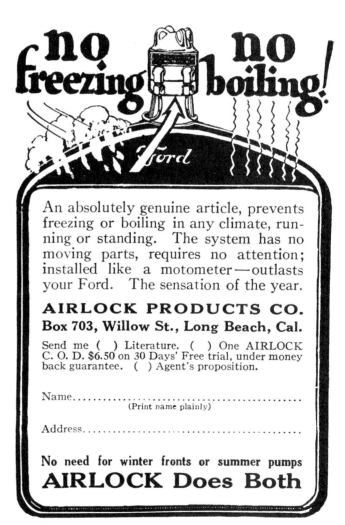

A 1925 ad for an add-on feature that promised to prevent not only engine overheating but freezing, apparently without the use of antifreeze. It seems to be a device which allowed the escape of water approaching the boiling point, which would also have allowed water approaching the freezing point to ooze out, possibly preventing a cracked block or radiator. Its value, however, would seem questionable at best.

Water, seventy percent; alcohol and glycerine, thirty percent; freezes at five degrees Fahrenheit below zero.

Water, sixty percent; alcohol and glycerine, forty percent; freezes at twenty-three degrees Fahrenheit below zero.

The proper proportions to be used must of course be governed by local conditions, but it is better to be safe than sorry, and make the solutions strong enough for any extreme that may be expected.

After due care has been taken with the cooling system to prevent freezing, the next point to observe is the lubrication of the motor. This will depend on the grades of oil which are normally employed. As a general rule it is well to use a lighter grade in winter.

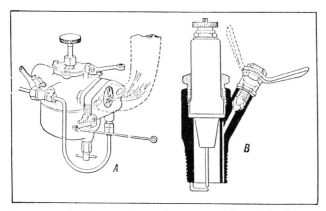

Devices to facilitate cold-weather starts. A is an Injex Primer. B is a special plug with a priming valve attachment.

The Blancke Automatic Carburetor Control for cold-weather starting.

If an acetylene lighting system utilizing a gas generator is fitted, it is necessary that the water used in the tank or the water jacket provided on some generators, be drained off and replaced with a solution of denatured alcohol and water of the proper consistency for the temperature liable to be met with.

During cold weather, a certain amount of difficulty is always experienced in starting the car, especially when one considers the low grade of gasoline used at the present time. The Ford engine is not provided with petcocks through which gasoline may be ejected as in other automobiles. Special spark plugs may be obtained having a petcock incorporated with the plug body or a special primer may be placed between the carburetor and manifold.

Pulling a wire when cranking a car equipped with the primer permits gasoline to flow directly to the intake manifold. In extreme cold weather, many motorists disconnect the fan belt in order that the air draught through the radiator will not cool the water to such a point that the engine will not run efficiently. Other motorists provide some form of lined leather shield for the front of the radiator to minimize airflow.

The Ford lighting system

The system of lighting supplied with the Ford car includes three oil lamps, two at the dash and one at the rear. The headlights of models made previous to 1915 are of the acetylene gas burning type, deriving the gas from action of water on calcium carbide in a simple generator carried on the running boards. A special form of burner is used in the Ford automobile headlights, which mixes a certain amount of air with the gas and the brilliant white light produced is intensified and projected by means of a lens mirror placed at the back of the lamp.

This lens provides great illuminating power which will light up the road for several hundred feet and permit higher speeds with safety than would be possible with the feeble glimmer of oil lamps.

The generator employed and its mode of operation may be easily understood. It consists of a water tank and separate compartments for carbide. As soon as the

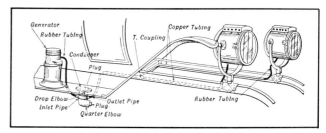

Acetylene lighting system similar to that used for Model T lights on 1910 to 1914 models.

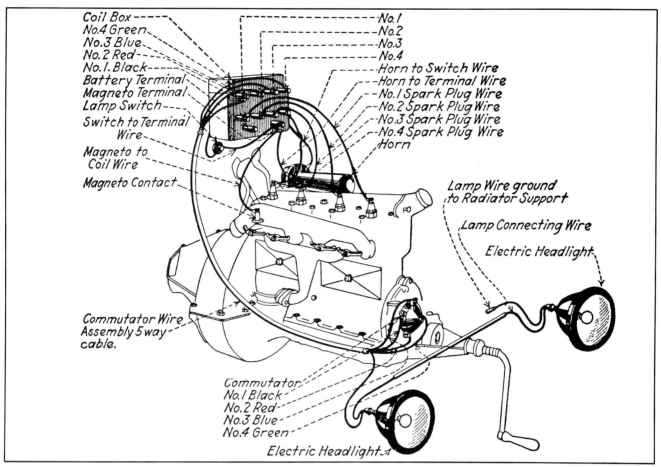

Coil Box
No.4 Green
No.3 Blue
No.2 Red
No.1 Black
Battery Terminal
Magneto Terminal
Lamp Switch
Switch to Terminal
Wire
Magneto to
Coil Wire
Magneto Contact

No.1
No.2
No.3
No.4
Horn to Switch Wire
Horn to Terminal Wire
No.1 Spark Plug Wire
No.2 Spark Plug Wire
No.3 Spark Plug Wire
No.4 Spark Plug Wire
Horn

Lamp Wire ground
to Radiator Support

Lamp Connecting Wire

Electric Headlight

Commutator Wire
Assembly 5 way
cable.

Commutator
No.1 Black
No.2 Red
No.3 Blue
No.4 Green

Electric Headlight

Model T ignition system with magneto current used to power
headlights.

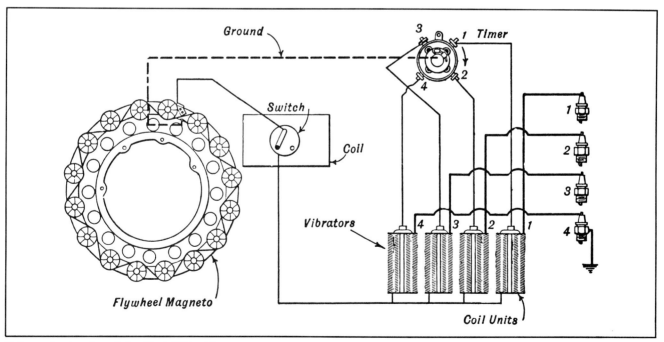

Schematic drawing of the Model T ignition system.

two come into contact, acetylene gas is produced, with lime dust collecting at the bottom of the generator as a residue. The gas is cooled before it reaches the lamps by the outlet pipe, surrounded by water. The generator must be cleaned after every trip in which it was used.

A 1924 ad offering a complete lighting system for the Model T using a generator as a power source.

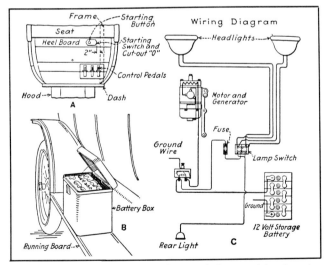

Drawing showing the original use of the combined motor starter-generator and placement of dry cells when these were used to facilitate dynamo starting.

Electric lighting for Ford cars

Many owners of Ford cars have fitted electric lights instead of the kerosene lamps and gas lights furnished up to this year. A number of attachments have been offered, designed to fit the gas headlights. Previous to 1915, the Ford Motor Company did not recommend the use of magneto current for electric lighting inasmuch as it was stated that this interfered with ignition. The Ford magneto has been redesigned with larger magnets, thus producing more power, now sufficient to power the electric lights.

As electrical lighting is now common on all other makes of cars, many owners of earlier Fords have fitted their cars with electric lighting systems available on the open market. The writer desired to use electric side and tail lamps instead of oil lamps regularly furnished, but owing to a warning of the manufacturer of the car, no attempt was made to utilize magneto current for this purpose. Instead, a 6-volt, 80-ampere hour storage battery was installed under the rear seat to furnish the power. This has proved thoroughly prac-

A 1918 ad offering complete electrical lighting for the Model T using a generator. Note interesting copy offering a light for the speedometer and a special spotlight.

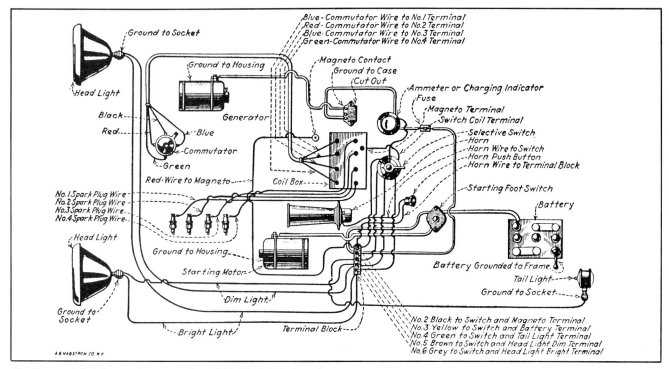

Starting and lighting systems on the 1918 Model T closed body cars, also used on all 1919-20 models. Note the use of a separate generator and starting motor.

tical as it was only necessary to charge the battery once a month.

The application of a simple fitting to convert the square oil side light to an electric side light had an ad-

vantage, inasmuch as the oil burner could be used in the event of failure of the electrical current. The tail light is practically the same as the original design, except that it is smaller and has a red lens instead of the

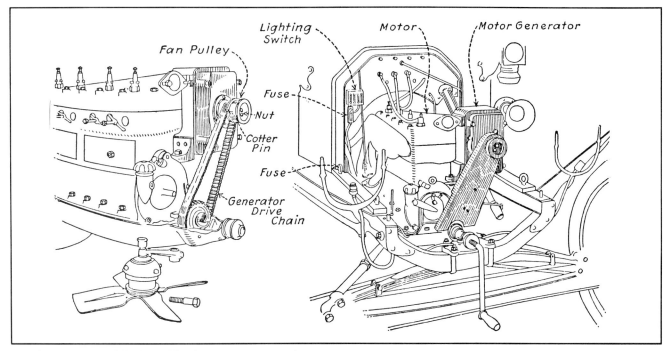

Drawing showing original combined starter-generator, location and means of being driven.

white one. If electric lights are installed, the current being taken from the magneto will be sufficient, with the larger magneto.

Ford electric starting system

There is a demand for self-starting systems of the electrical type, and when such a system is provided it is possible to use electric side lights and tail lights as well as headlights. In the regular Ford lighting system, the lamps go out when the engine is stopped and burn dimly when the engine runs slowly. Because of this, the side lamps burn kerosene oil.

When a starting system is fitted, a storage battery is installed and lights may be had regardless of engine speed. A variety of simple starting and lighting systems have been designed for Ford cars. One combines the starter and generator and is driven by a silent chain.

When the engine turns the dynamo, it generates current which is stored in the battery. When the engine is stopped, current from the battery is used to power the starter when it is used.

A 1915 ad by still another firm offering a starting and lighting system for the Model T.

A 1917 ad for an unusual starter for the Model T. This type utilized a combination spring-leverage system which utilized the force built up to turn over the engine.

The starting and lighting systems on 1919 and 1920 Fords are of the two-unit type and consists of a starting motor, generator, storage battery, charging indicator and lights, together with the necessary wiring and connections shown in one of the drawings. The starting motor is mounted on the left-hand side of the engine and bolted to the transmission cover. When in operation, the pinion on the Bendex drive shaft engages with the teeth on the flywheel.

The spark and throttle levers should be placed in the same positions on the quadrant as when cranking by hand. Current from either battery or magneto may be used for starting. When starting, especially if the engine is cold, the ignition switch should be turned to "battery." As soon as the engine is warmed up, turn switch back to "magneto." The magneto was designed to furnish ignition for the Model T engine and better results are obtained if attention is paid to the position of the spark lever, as a too advanced spark will cause serious backfiring which in turn, will bend or break the shaft of the starter.

The starting motor is operated by a push button, conveniently located on the floor of the car at the driver's feet. With the spark and throttle levers in the proper positions, and the ignition switch turned on, press on the push button with the foot. This closes the circuit, turning over the crank shaft.

When the engine is cold it may be necessary to prime it by pulling out the carburetor priming rod, which is located on the instrument board. In order to avoid flooding the engine with an over-rich mixture of gas, the priming rod should only be held out for a few seconds at a time.

If the engine fails to start with the above procedure, release the button at once, and inspect the carburetor and ignition systems. First inspect the terminals on the starting motor. If they are tight, examine the rest of the wiring for a break in the insulation which would result in a short circuiting. Next, test the battery with a hydrometer. A reading of less than 1.225 indicates a run-down battery, which may be the cause of the trouble.

Operation of the generator

The generator is mounted on the right-hand side of the engine and is bolted to the cylinder front end cover. It is operated by the pinion on the armature shaft engaging with the large timing gear. The charging rate is designed to set in at 10 miles per hour, reaching a maximum charging rate at 20 miles per hour. At higher car speeds, the charge will taper off by the actions of the cut-out, which is set by the factory and should not be tampered with under any circumstances. Both the starting motor and the generator are properly lubricated at the factory via a designed-in system and re-

quire no attention on the part of the operator, except for a few drops of oil which can be supplied via the oil cup at the end of the generator housing.

The introduction of a battery current into the magneto system will discharge the magnets, so, when-

A 1923 ad for an alternate fuse block for the Model T, permitting the "use of single filament lamps for bright and dim lights." The system also eliminated flickering lights caused by varying magneto voltage and blown-out "lamps" due to this excessive voltage.

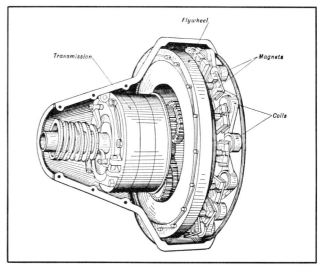

Drawing of the original magneto showing the three clutches needed to get low, high and reverse gear with epicyclic transmission.

A 1925 ad for the Spad timer, guaranteed to eliminate Model T bucking, jerking, misfiring and sputtering. It was made of bakelight—"There can be no short circuit, nor oiling needed." Replacement timers were one of the most frequently advertised Model T items.

ever repairing the ignition system or tampering with the electrical wiring in any way, do not fail to disconnect the positive wire from the battery. The end of this wire should be wound with tape to prevent its coming into contact with any portion of the car.

Regarding the home wiring of headlights, the usual method is to run a wire from the magneto terminal to a one-point switch on the dash, then from the switch to one side of the left headlight double contact bulb. The headlight bulb is then connected to its neighbor, the free terminal of which is grounded to the frame side member. This means that the lights are wired in series, enabling the use of the six or seven volt bulbs which are standard, easily procured and at the same time, insures against burning them out at high speed. If the headlights are connected to the storage battery, they should be wired in multiple instead of series, just as the side lamps. Separate switches should be provided for the headlights, side lights and tail lamp circuits, inasmuch as it is not necessary to use all the lamps at the same time. While the tail light must be kept burning all the time, it can be used in connection with the side lamps for city driving and these can be extinguished and only the headlights used for cross country driving.

The Ford magneto

A very ingenious and practical application of the dynamo is used on Ford cars only. The electric generator is built in such a manner that it forms an integral part of the power plant. The electrical field (current) is produced by a series of revolving permanent magnets which are joined to and turn with the flywheel. The sixteen current-producing coils are carried by a fixed plate which is attached to the engine base. This apparatus is really having a revolving field and a fixed armature, and with this arrangement, there is no connecting arrangement to get out of order.

The coils in which the current is generated are stationary, no rotating commutators or fixed contact brushes are needed to collect the current because the electricity may be easily taken from the fixed coils by a simple direct connection. It has been suggested that this type of magneto is not as efficient as the conventional patterns because more metal and wire are needed to produce the required voltage. As the magnets form the heaviest portion of the system, and are attached to the flywheel, they merely add to the flywheel weight and so suffer no serious defect. As already pointed out, additional voltage or amperage can be obtained merely by increasing the size of the magnets. Another advantage is, as long as the engine is turning over, you have voltage, something that can't be said for a battery.

Many owners provide a set of dry cells as an auxiliary source of current, as these are of value in starting the engine sometimes under conditions where the engine cannot be cranked briskly enough to get the magneto to give a good spark. Dry cells are useful also as a check on the magneto and are also of value when adjusting the coil vibrators. The engine will also start on the spark sometimes without cranking when dry cells are used.

The author operated his Model T for two seasons with the magneto alone, without a battery, and never felt the need for one. It was only when a storage battery was added to the equipment to operate electric side and tail lamps that the battery terminal of the coil was put into the circuit, though it was seldom used.

The master vibrator system

One of the most widely advertised accessories intended for use on the Ford car is called a "master vibrator." This consists of a very simple primary coil carrying a vibrator intended to serve all the coil units, the regular vibrators with which these are provided being shorted out. Opinions regarding the practical utility of a master vibrator differ greatly, some contending that it materially improves the steady operation of the engine, while others believe it has no material advantage over the factory system.

The contention made by those favoring the device is that the use of one vibrator for all coil units provides a spark that will occur in each cylinder at exactly the same time, because it reduces the lag that might result from tardy action of one or more of the individual unit coil vibrators. The argument of greater simplicity via the use of only one vibrator is the more reasonable one.

The writer has not found it necessary to adopt the single vibrator method, inasmuch as he has never had any trouble with the factory-equipped system, it requiring only a few minutes to adjust any of the on-board coil vibrators, when such work was occasionally necessary. The non-mechanical Ford owner who cannot adjust the factory-equipped vibrators, is not apt to have much success in adjusting one faulty vibrator, whereas if only one of the four coil units is not working properly, or not adjusted properly, the engine will still function with some degree of efficiency on the other three units.

The Ford float feed carburetor

The modern form of spraying carburetor is provided with two chambers through which the air stream passes and mixes with a gasoline spray, the other a float chamber in which a constant level of fuel is maintained by a simple mechanism. A nozzle or its equivalent is used in the mixing chamber to spray the fuel through and the object of the float is to maintain the fuel level to such a point that it will not overflow when the engine is not drawing in a charge of gas.

Two different carburetors are used on the Model T. The action is the same in both types, except that one has an auxiliary air attachment consisting of a series of bronze balls which open progressively as the engine suction increases to admit more air into the mixture. Ford carburetors have but one adjustment, the so-called needle valve. The fuel enters the float bowl through a side connection, its level there being regulated by a cork float. The float rises as the gasoline in-

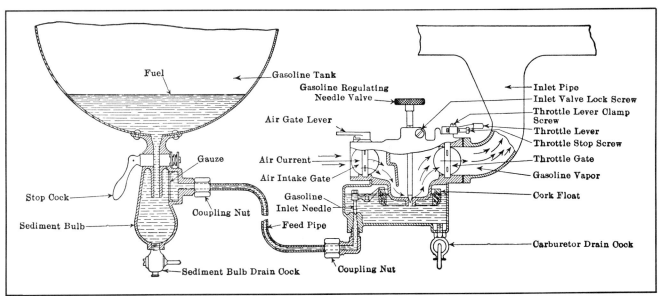

The original Model T fuel system, requiring no vacuum tank or fuel pump. The gas tank was located under the front seat, allowing gas to flow easily to the carburetor located slightly below the tank. The car sometimes had difficulty climbing steep hills, when the carburetor would fail to draw gas because of its higher position.

A 1928 ad for a Model T carburetor add-on to increase mileage to phenomenal lengths. It also "starts Ford instantly . . . eliminates oil pumping in front cylinder . . . (and produces) complete combustion." Just how the device did all this was never explained.

creases to the point where the supply is regulated by a valve, eventually cutting off the gas flow. As the gas is used up and the amount in the bowl becomes less, the float drops and via a bell crank lifts the needle from its seat, permitting more gas to enter the bowl.

A constant level of gasoline in the float chamber is thus maintained. The actual amount of gasoline involved in the mixture is determined by the setting of the needle valve. A mixture that contains too much air is known as a "lean" mixture. If it contains too much raw gasoline, it is called a "rich" mixture. Neither one of these conditions is desirable, as the engine will be hard to start and also lack power on a lean mixture as well as having a tendency to overheat. An over rich mixture will tend to promote carbon deposits in the cylinder.

A rich mixture is indicated by a heavy black exhaust smoke having a disagreeable smell. When this condition is manifested, the needle valve regulator on the dash should be screwed to the right, until the engine begins to misfire, then the gasoline feed is gradually increased by opening up the needle valve in the other direction slowly to that point where the motor runs steadily and there is no more black exhaust visible. White smoke coming out of the exhaust pipe indicates too much lubricating oil and too little gas combination. If popping sounds are heard in the carburetor, it is because the mixture is too thin and the needle valve should be opened up just enough to permit the engine to run well and yet not backfire.

Ford water circulation by natural system

Some engineers contend that the rapid water circulation obtained by using a pump may cool the cylinders

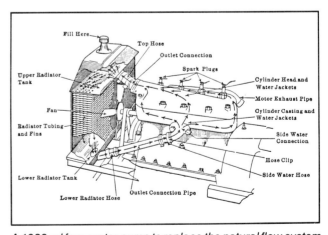

The Model T thermo-siphon water cooling system, abandoned today as ineffective with modern high-powered engines. When originally adopted, the T had a 4:1 compression ratio and a 20 hp "modern" engine.

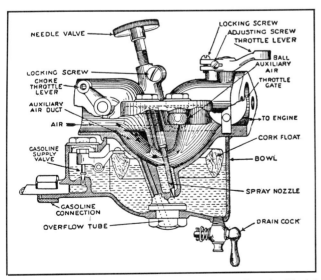

Sectional view of the Kingston carburetor used on the Model T.

A 1922 ad for a water pump to replace the natural flow system provided by the factory. Many firms offered such water pumps, all of which provided better service than the original system which caused the engine to overheat under difficult circumstances.

79

too much, so that efficiency will be reduced. For this reason there is a growing tendency to use the natural method of water circulation as the cooling liquid is supplied to the cylinder jackets just below the boiling point, and the water issues from the jacket at the top of the cylinder after it has absorbed sufficient heat to raise it just about to the boiling point.

The Ford system is very successful in practice, and is somewhat simpler than the forms in which a pump is used to maintain circulation. With this method, the fact that water becomes lighter as its temperature rises is taken advantage of in securing circulation around the cylinders. The top of the water jacket of the block cast cylinder head is attached to the top center of the radiator, while the pipe leading from the bottom of that member is connected to a manifold which supplies cool water to the bottom of the cylinder jacket.

With a thermo-siphon system, it is imperative that the radiator be carried at such a height that the cool water will flow to the water spaces around the cylinder by gravity. As the water becomes heated by contact with the hot cylinder and combustion cylinder walls it rises to the top of the cylinders, flows to the cooler, where enough of the heat is absorbed to cause it to become greater in weight.

As the water becomes cooler, it falls to the bottom of the radiator and is again supplied to the water jacket. The circulation is entirely automatic and continues as long as there is a difference in temperature between the liquid in the cooler and that in the jacket. The circulation becomes brisker as the engine becomes hotter and thus the temperature of the cylinders is kept nearly to a fixed point.

With the thermo-siphon system, the cooling liquid is nearly always at its boiling point, whereas if the circulation is maintained by a pump, the engine will become cooler at high speed and will heat up more at low speed. So long as the proper quantity of water is used in the radiator, there is nothing that will interfere with proper engine cooling. There is no pump drive to complicate the construction and require attention. It is an ideal cooling system for a car designed for use by the masses.

How the Ford power plant is lubricated

The system of lubrication employed in the Ford power plant is an exceptionally simple one, requiring no apparatus other than that regularly forming a part of the engine. The magneto magnets attached to the flywheel rim also serve as a portion of the lubricating system in circulating engine oil. A series of troughs is placed on the center line of each cylinder in the bottom plate, these being arranged so that as the connecting rods rotate, the big ends dip into the troughs and scoop out some of the oil present in these members, throwing it about the engine interior and lubricating all parts exposed to the spray. It will be evident that all internal parts of the engine will be oiled continuously, if some means is provided for keeping these troughs or channels full of oil.

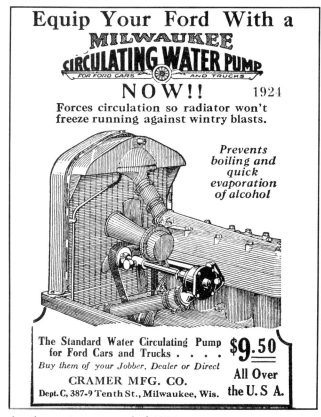

Another water pump ad of 1924.

The above gadget of 1926 was used to help solve overheating problems of the Model T. The item ffered the driver a warning: "Red spot flashes when water boils." It also served to indicate when the radiator needed water.

This object is attained in a very simple manner by filling the flywheel compartment of the engine crank case to a definite height which is indicated by small drain cocks placed on the back side of the lower crank case compartment. This level is sufficiently high so the magnets are partially submerged in the oil as the flywheel revolves. It will be apparent that considerable oil will be scooped up by the projecting magnets, and these are utilized to lift oil into a small funnel attached to the side of the crank case and in the path of the oil stream.

This funnel communicates with a brass tube that conveys the stream of lubricating oil to the front crank case compartment housing the timing gears. From this point, the oil drains back, filling the troughs until they overflow, the surplus then flowing back into the flywheel compartment of the crank case. This system of lubrication provides for a thorough lubricity of the exposed planetary transmission gears carried in the gear case, which really forms the rear part of the engine crank case.

The oil is introduced into the engine through an opening obtained by removing the brass cover of the breather pipe. When the Ford engine is new and all crank case joints are tight, there is no leakage, and oil consumption will be equivalent to about one quart per hundred miles of car operation. The car makers advise keeping the oil level at a point about midway between the two petcocks, but how this can be determined without the use of the X-ray can only be conjectured.

They advise that carrying the oil level above the top petcock will result in excessive use of oil, whereas, having the level below the lower petcock will be apt to result injuriously, owing to lack of adequate lubrication. However, it is better to use too much oil than not enough, so most Ford owners fill the flywheel compartment to the height indicated by the top drain cock. Simple glass gauge fittings may be procured from accessory dealers by which the height of the oil may be accurately gauged. These replace the lower petcock, and many Ford owners find it desirable to purchase this inexpensive fitting, as the level of the oil may be determined at a glance.

During practically all the time that the writer had his Model T in operation, it was his rule to supply one quart of oil through the breather pipe for every five gallons of gasoline put into the gas tank, as previously mentioned. Then, the top petcock was opened until the surplus lubricant had drained out. With the Ford system of lubrication, it is necessary to remove the crank case oil plug at the bottom of the flywheel compartment and drain out the old oil at least every five hundred miles, flushing out the interior of the crank case thoroughly with gasoline or kerosene and introducing

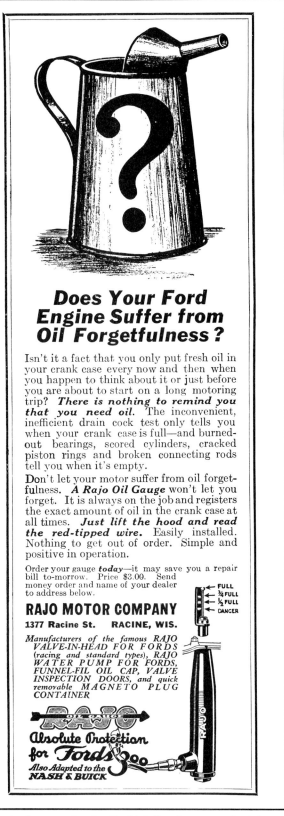
A 1922 oil gauge for the T which "is always on the job and registers the exact amount of oil in the crankcase at all times." The gauge was mounted on the engine. Note statement that it was adopted by both Nash and Buick.

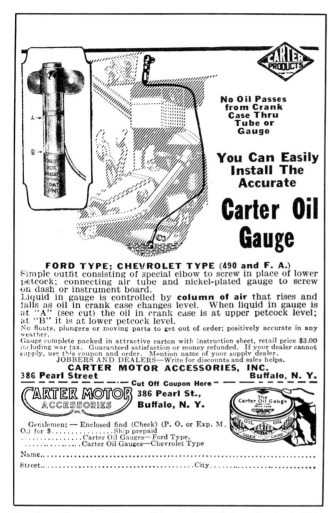

Another oil gauge offering, this one installed on the dash. This one seems to have worked on the same principle as the gas gauge on the Model A. Too bad Ford didn't adopt it on the Model T; it was a simple, sound idea.

enough lubricant after the oil plug has been replaced, to bring the level of the fresh oil to the proper height.

Why change speed gearing is needed

Those who are familiar with steam or electricity as a source of power for motor vehicles may not understand the necessity for the change speed gearing which is such an essential component of the automobile propelled by internal combustion engines. In explaining the reason for the use of the clutch it has been demon-

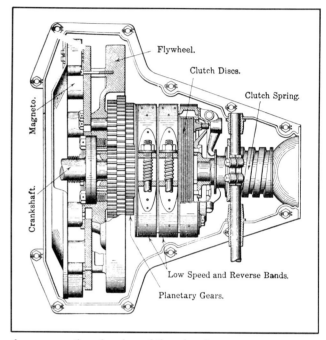

A cross-section drawing of the planetary gear arrangement detailing the magneto and clutch discs.

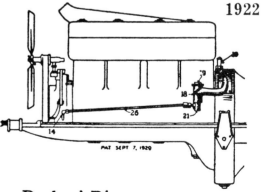

A 1922 ad offering a replacement oil and filter combo, said to contain no moving parts and would last "indefinitely." It worked in conjunction with the Model T's splash system. The only advantage seems to have been the device's ability to supply oil from a reservoir "regardless of the speed of the motor."

strated that steam or electric motors are very flexible and that their speed does not actually determine their power output, which can be regulated by the amount of energy supplied from the boiler or the battery.

In short, more voltage may be applied to an electric motor, within limits it is designed for, of course, and in the steam engine, more pressure can be released into the cylinder. In each case, this results in more power being developed. A steam engine, in fact, develops its greatest power at *zero* r.p.m. In an explosion engine, as they used to be called, we can increase the power after the maximum pressure has been reached, only by increasing the engine's speed. Whereas it is possible to couple a steam engine or an electric motor directly to the drive wheels of an automobile, it is not possible to do this with gasoline engines. Some form of gearing is obviously necessary in order that the engine can be made to run at the speed needed to develop the power required to move the vehicle, consistent with the requirements of the moment. Additionally, while both d.c. electric motors and steam engines can be made to reverse themselves, an internal combustion engine requires special gears for that operation.

How planetary gearing operates

The planetary epicycle transmission is an easily operated form of speed change gear that has been very popular on small cars. This system has many features of merit. It provides a positive drive, and, as the gears are always in mesh, these gears cannot be damaged by careless shifting. Individual clutches are used for speed selection, and as the operation of the clutch occurs at the same time that the desired speed is selected, any of the various speed changes desired may be easily effected by the manipulation of a single hand lever or pedal.

The planetary gearing system used on the Ford car operates as follows: This system contains only spur pinions. The flywheel web serves as pinion carrier and driving member, having three lateral studs secured into it which carry triple planetary pinions. The main gear is the driving member, being keyed to the clutch drum, which in turn is secured to the driven shaft. By applying a brake band to either of the rotating forward drums, or to the reverse drum, the car can be made to move either forward, at the low speed or high speed, or made to reverse.

Planetary gearing has been very successful when the system is properly designed and installed. Its chief disadvantage is that it is very difficult to provide more than two forward speeds and one reverse. It is for this reason that it can only be adopted on light cars having a surplus of power for the size and weight of the car, as in the Model T Ford. While such gearing is not as efficient as a progressive-type of transmission at least

in low and reverse gears, as considerable power is absorbed in friction, it is superior in direct or high gear, as the entire assembly is locked to the crank shaft. No gears turn idly and the weight of the gearing serves merely as additional flywheel weight.

Considerable trouble was experienced with early forms of planetary gearing before being adopted by

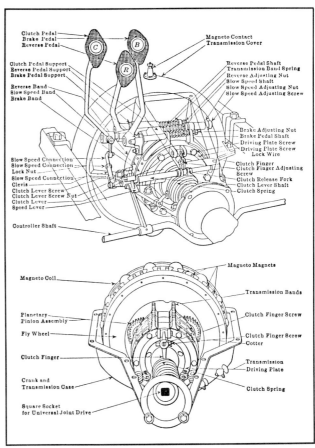

A factory drawing of the transmission system of the T showing control pedals and other related mechanisms at top and partially disassembled brake bands and related parts at bottom.

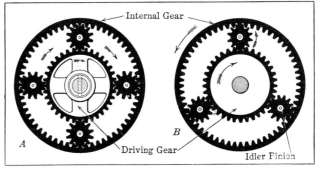

Drawings demonstrating action of the epicyclic gearing. At A is the slow-speed gear assembly. At B are the gears and pinions used in the reverse drive.

Ford, as it proved difficult to keep the crank case from leaking. In the Ford design, special care has been taken in housing the reduction gears so that these are constantly oiled and so that both wear and noise, which were formerly detrimental to the adoption of planetary gearing, have been largely eliminated.

Adjusting the transmission

If any difficulty is experienced in climbing hills in high gear and the engine seems to be delivering its normal power, it is because the high speed clutch is slipping. If the engine races when the slow speed pedal is pushed up as tight as it will go when climbing steep hills, it is because the slow speed band needs adjusting. Should the car show a tendency to creep forward when the crank is turned, this indicates that the clutch lever screw which bears on the clutch lever cam is worn and requires an extra turn down to hold the clutch in neutral position.

The screw passes through the boss on the end of a simple lever, the other end of which is joined to the clutch actuating pedal by a simple rod and yoke connection. The lock nut must be released before attempting to screw down the clutch lever screw. Care must be taken not to screw it down any further than necessary or the high speed clutch will slip.

To make adjustments to the reverse or transmission brake band, or to the high speed clutch, the plate on the transmission cover must be removed. It will be necessary to remove the floor boards to get at this portion of the power plant. It will be noticed that there are three clutch fingers spaced around the front end of the transmission drum. These have set screws which are prevented from turning by split pin locks. If the high speed clutch is slipping, the split pin on the clutch finger that locks the set screw should be removed and the set screw given one-half or one complete turn to the right with a screw driver. Each of the other set screws

A 1926 ad for Ford replacement transmission bands, touting much superior bands "made of chemically processed, scientifically constructed, selected wood (instead of the old style easy-to-burn-out fabric)." The grooved, heavily lubricated strips of asbestos provided "an extremely powerful grip . . . yet a smoothness that is non-chattering." The claims proved to be debatable.

should be turned exactly the same amount, then replace the locking split pin.

The low speed band may be tightened without removing the transmission plate cover. Turn the adjusting screw to the right until appreciable resistance is felt when the clutch pedal is pushed way forward. Care should be taken not to tighten the bands too much, as they may drag on the transmission drum assembly at high speed, act as a brake and tend to overheat the engine.

The reverse band should be tightened in the same way. If the friction linings of the bands are worn to such an extent that adjusting the brake does not seem to improve matters, they should be removed and relined with new friction material. Linings are expensive but with good care, a set of reverse and slow speed bands should last at least 10,000 miles, and foot brakes over 5,000 miles.

Utility of motor-car brakes

There are three brakes provided on the Ford chassis, one of these being a service brake acting on the transmission gear, the other two being emergency members acting on the drums carried by the rear wheels.

The transmission brake is the one normally used when driving the car and is operated by the right hand pedal. When this pedal is pushed forward, it constricts an asbestos fabric lined brake band around the drum that also forms the casing for the multiple disc clutch assembly.

As this drum is part of the assembly to which the propeller shaft is attached and as this in turn controls the rear wheels through the medium of the bevel pinion carried at its lower end, whenever the transmission assembly is gripped by this brake band, it will also retard the movement of the rear wheels and if the brake pedal is pushed tightly enough, the friction will be so great that the rear wheels cannot turn and must come to a stop, even on a steep incline. This is called the "service brake" because it is more generally used than the hand operated brake acting directly on the rear wheel drums.

The emergency brake consists of a pair of semicircular cast iron shoe members held together against an anchorage pin and an expanding cam by coil springs. The diameter of the circle formed by these two metal shoes is slightly less than the inside diameter of the brake drum when the brake is not in use. If the hub brake is rocked, however, so that instead of lying flat, it is moved at such an angle that the brake shoes are spread apart, they will grip the internal periphery of the pressed steel brake drum, retarding or entirely stopping the wheels, depending upon the pressure applied by the hand lever and the movement of the actuat-

ing cam. As soon as the pressure is released, the coil springs release the brake shoes from contacting the drum, permitting free rotation of the wheel.

The emergency brake linkage is interconnected with the clutch actuating pedal so that when the handle is placed in a certain position, the clutch will disengage but the brakes will not be brought into action until a further movement of the hand lever takes place. The handle may be locked in any desired position by a simple ratchet and pawl arrangement at its lower end.

This is a good feature, as the emergency brake may be applied to prevent the car from moving when

A 1924 ad offering superior brakes that had withstood a "user test." While the material may have resulted in a better brake, as author Victor Page points out, the Ford brakes were actually too small themselves and so it is doubtful if any superior brake band could have been any more effective as far as stopping distance was concerned; though a longer life, maybe.

the engine is being cranked or when it is left unattended on a grade. The service brake may be operated at the same time as the emergency brakes are, if desired, though it is only on very steep hills that both brakes can be used to advantage.

Model T conversion sets

Another development worthy of mention is the large sale of adapters, special rear axles, auxiliary frames, etc., devised to transport a popular light-weight pleasure car into a one-ton capacity truck. These have not been used under varying conditions long enough yet to determine their real value and influence on the depreciation of the power-producing elements of the original chassis, which have not been strengthened proportionally as the load-carrying members have. These can be divided into five general classes:

(1) Those that retain the Ford rear axle and spring, but in which the wheel base is increased by the introduction of a section in the frame and in which the drive shaft is also increased in length to correspond to the increased wheel base;

(2) Those that provide for additional load capacity by the use of supplementary springs attached directly to the housings of the drive gearing actuating the steel wheel. These wheels are carried on special bearings independent of the Ford rear axle, so this member is used merely to transmit power and is not subjected to the strain of carrying the vehicle load;

(3) In this class, the rear axle is used for a jack-shaft for a chain-driven rear-end truck assembly, which is a unit with a supplementary frame extension adapted to be easily attached to the regular chassis;

(4) This type is similar, except that the rear axle is changed into a jackshaft for an internal gear-driven unit. Instead of sprockets on the axle shaft ends, as in (3), spur pinions which mesh with large internal spur gears driving the wheels, are employed;

(5) In this type, an auxiliary frame extension is used, but this carries a worm or internal gear drive axle as well as special springs and wheels. The regular Ford rear axle is not used at all, nor are the Ford rear wheels. Those types in which the load is carried on special springs and axle members (2–5), are much stronger than those in (1). The regular rear end construction was never intended to carry heavy loads.

It will be evident from all this, that there is a considerable number of conversion units available for the Model T, to convert it into a commercial vehicle. (Originally published in 1915; revised and republished in 1916, 1917, 1918, 1920, 1923, 1926 and 1928.)

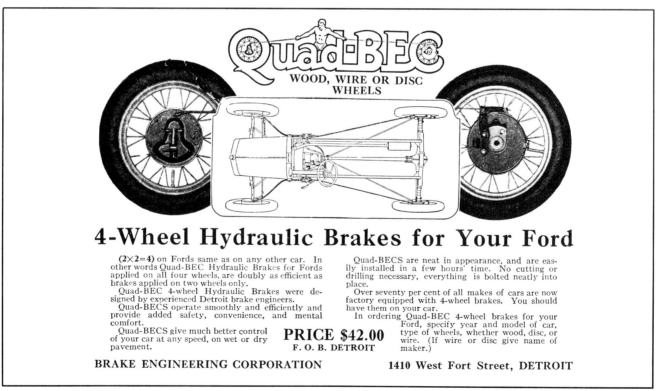

Here is the one really superior Model T brake offering—a four-wheel hydraulic brake system offered in 1926. Even the Model A didn't have that feature.

Chapter 6

Magazine Suggestions for Improving Your Model T

Wherein do-it-yourself inventions and conversions to better the Ford are offered by magazine writers and readers

Making gravity feed efficient

Failure of the gasoline to get into the carburetor when the car ascends a steep grade is a difficulty frequently experienced by owners of Ford cars. This trouble can be prevented to a great extent by simply lowering the carburetor from the position indicated by the dotted lines, to a position about four inches below, and cutting and bending and fitting the tube to correspond. Such a shift necessitates the use of an offset extension to connect the carburetor to the intake manifold, which can be made from a short length of iron pipe provided with a flange of ⅜-in. flat iron to each end.

The extension must, of course, be fitted tightly and gaskets used where connection is made to the carburetor and manifold. If this arrangement is not desired, the same results can be accomplished by providing a small hand air pump below the front seat, and connecting this to the gas tank, as shown. The most convenient location for the pump is at the right side of the driver's seat.
(*Popular Mechanics*, June 1925)

Oil cooler for Model T Ford

It is an easy matter to make an effective oil cooler for your Model T Ford, from a length of copper tubing and two fittings, which will prevent the oil from thinning out on long or fast drives, and thus supply a quantity of cool oil to the valve chamber reservoir at all times.

Demonstrating the automatic oil feed.

The oil-line plug directly below the carburetor is removed and an L-fitting inserted. A ¼-in. hole is drilled and tapped in the valve chamber cover, about 1-in. from the right edge, and an I-fitting installed. About 8 turns of ¼-in. copper are wound in a 5 or 6-in. spiral. A large thermos bottle will be found handy to use as a form for bending the tubing.
(*Popular Mechanics*, March 1925)

Shield keeps auto engine warm

It is necessary that your Ford be kept warm on cold days if you are using it. This can be done by obtaining a piece of metal lath of the kind shown in the photo, cutting it to fit over the front of the radiator and attaching with a couple of stove bolts. This, when painted black, will have the appearance of a winter front that has been purchased at some accessory store and will answer the purpose almost as well. It allows enough air to enter but the engine cannot overheat on a cold day.
(*Popular Mechanics*, June 1927)

Preserving Model T Ford bands

Ford Model T bands are designed to operate in a bath of oil. The band linings are porous strips of cotton material especially woven and prepared for the work of clutching the drums for low speed and reverse, and also for use in braking the car.

When the car is being driven along the roadway in high gear there is a constant bath of engine oil falling onto the bands and this finds its way into the fabric of the band linings, completely soaking them. In descending a long hill, the brake pedal is sometimes held down tightly for long periods. Holding the brake down stead-

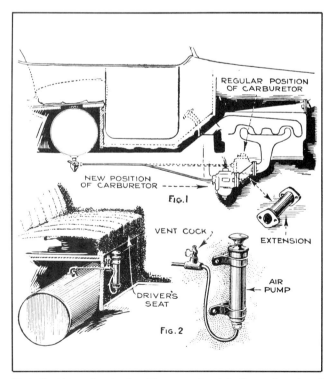

Two simple methods of getting gasoline into the carburetor of a gravity-feed car when ascending steep grades.

Copper coil installed on a Ford motor keeps oil cool on long and fast drives.

ily will result in burning the band lining and glazing. This will result in the band looking like charcoal. A band lining in this condition is useless.

The driver may put a band lining "out of commission" on a single hill. Or a good driver may preserve the bands in good condition indefinitely by careful driving procedure. What is the secret of proper driving procedure? you ask. It is very simple in operation and principle. In the first place, release the foot brake every little distance in descending a long hill. This allows more oil to find its way into the lining to saturate it, cool it, and keep it fit. If the hill is long, use reverse in conjunction with the brake. While one band is cooling and being lubricated, the other checks the speed of the car.

(*Modern Mechanix and Inventions*, July 1929)

Heater for the Ford

During cold weather it is often desired to have a heater in the car. A good one for the Ford sedan can be made in the following way: A length of ordinary galvanized-iron conductor pipe, about 40-in. long, has a hole, 3-in. square cut in it about 2-in. from one end. Slip the conductor over the exhaust pipe in the position indicated, just ahead of the muffler. The hole in the conductor pipe should then be directly under the floorboards behind the front seat.

Both ends of the conductor are securely wired to the muffler and exhaust pipe. A short length of square conductor, cut to fit snugly over the hole in the round

one, is attached vertically, the upper end projecting through a hole cut in the floorboards.

A piece of heavy wire mesh is tacked down on the floorboard over the opening, and the floor mat is cut to

A 1924 ad for Ford bands, catering to do-it-yourself car owners.

A radiator cover for cold weather can be made from metal lath.

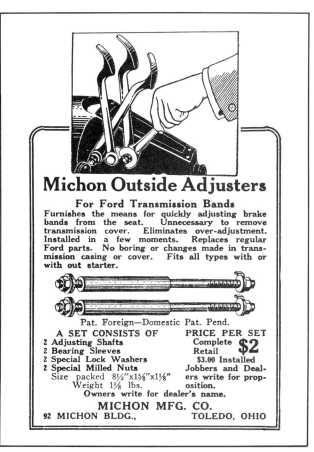

Another ad from 1922 for home mechanics to do their own adjusting on Ford bands.

correspond. If too much heat comes out, the cut-out section can be slipped back in place over the opening. In use, the air enters the front end of the conductor pipe, is warmed by coming in contact with the hot exhaust pipe, and is conducted into the car. The rear end of the pipe should be closed by butting it against the muffler or by filling it with asbestos paper, for a considerable amount of warm air will otherwise be lost at this point.

(*Popular Mechanics*, January 1928)

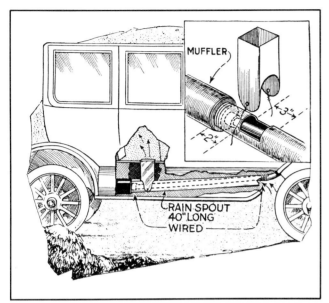

Efficient homemade exhaust pipe heater for a Ford sedan can be made from conductor pipe.

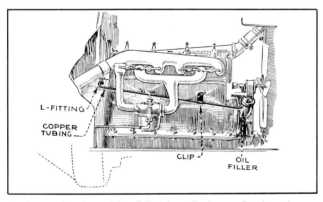

An improvised outside oil line installed on a Ford engine.

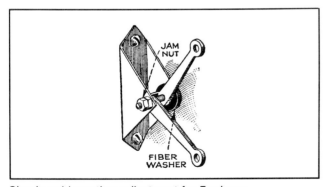

Simple cold weather adjustment for Ford cars.

Outside oil line on Ford motor makes quick repair

Some months ago, a Ford on which a connecting rod bearing cap had come loose was brought into the shop. Investigation showed that no harm had been done to the block or crankshaft and that a new connecting rod would easily remedy the matter. However, the oil pipe was crushed beyond repair, and the owners, a public utility company, would not permit the delay necessary to take the motor apart and install a new pipe.

I recalled having seen various outside oil lines for Ford motors, and here was a good case to use one. There was none on hand, but there was plenty of ¼-in. copper tubing and fittings, and a little thought showed me that a few feet of this tubing and an L-fitting would do the trick.

The transmission cover was removed and a hole drilled and tapped for the L-fitting about ½-in. to the right of the magneto plug and even with the back edge of the plug base. Care was exercised to tap the hole only so deep that the ell would fit tightly and not project beyond the inner surface of the cover. Some waste was then stuffed in the oil-filler opening to prevent any particles of metal from getting in, and a hole slightly smaller than the outside diameter of the copper tubing, drilled in the back side of the oil-filler casting, about ¾-in. from the top.

This hole was reamed out with a taper reamer until it was just large enough for the tubing. After this hole was finished, the waste and particles of metal were removed. With the transmission cover back in place, the tubing was bent to run from the L-fitting, around the

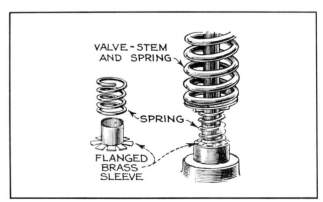

Means of eliminating Ford valve noise due to wearing of parts.

center of the block, along the right side of the motor under the exhaust pipe, carburetor, etc., to the hole drilled in the filler casting.

After allowing about ½-in. inside the filler opening, the piece was cut off and installed, care being exercised to see that the tube made a gradual slope to the front end of the motor. When the motor was ready for running, it was started at once, and the oil-filler cap was removed so that the results could be observed. A minute after the motor started the oil began to drop from the tube, and in another minute it had increased to a full flow. The principle of operation is this: Some of the oil in which the flywheel runs, is picked up and centrifugal force throws it off, a portion of it finding its way into the line of tubing, where gravity does the rest.

—Leon D. Quick, Milesburg, Pa.
(*Popular Mechanics*, December 1925)

Choking Fords in cold weather

An adjustable choker of the kind shown in the illustration has been devised for Ford automobiles, and found very satisfactory during cold weather. It can be made by removing the rivet from the original bracket and inserting a stove bolt in its place, with a fiber washer between the arms and the bracket proper. The tension on the bolt forces the choker to remain where it is set.

—R. Metayer, Alexandria, Va.
(*Popular Mechanics*, May 1924)

Silencing Ford valves

Valves on Fords and other motors which are of the non-adjustable type, become noisy after some use. Much of this noise is caused by wear on the end of the valve stem or tappet. It can be eliminated or absorbed by using a short length of thin brass tubing, just large enough to slip over the valve stem, and a coil spring a little larger in diameter than the tubing. With a fine-toothed hacksaw, the tubing is cut across the end in three or four places to a depth of ⅛-in. or a little more, care being taken to see that all the cuts are the same depth. The segments formed in this manner are bent out at straight angles to the wall of the tubing and the tube is cut off to a length of about ¼-in. Eight tubes, one for each valve stem, are required. The springs should be of fairly strong stock and should be cut about ¼-in. longer than the distance from the pinhole in the valve stem to the end of the stem.
(*Popular Mechanics*, June 1926)

Changing Ford clutch lever to foot control

The clutch or hand-brake lever on the Ford is seldom used for emergency stops, as it is in a very awkward position to reach in a hurry. The average owner simply uses it to throw the clutch into neutral and to

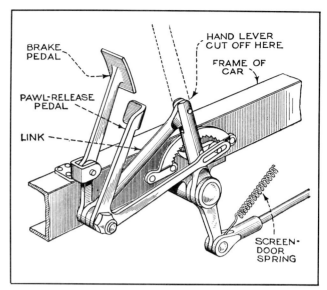

This simple attachment replaces the hand lever on the Ford car.

brake the car when at a standstill. By means of the simple attachment shown in the illustration, however, the hand lever is modified so that it can be applied with the foot without interfering with its clutch-releasing function.

If the emergency-brake bands are removed after this is done, and bands substituted that can be faced with brake lining as used on other cars, a double braking system is made that is very effective in emergencies. The change from the ordinary brake shoes is not essential, of course, but, as these wear out quickly under constant use, it will be found better in the end to make the change suggested.

The attachment consists of a pedal that actuates the rear brakes and releases the clutch at the same time. The hand-brake lever is cut off above the top of the pawl sector. A pedal is made of forged steel, to the shape shown, and pivoted on the frame forward of the brake lever. The top of the latter is slotted and drilled for a pin, and connected to the bottom of the pedal with a link. A forward movement of the foot throws the brake lever back, thus releasing the clutch and applying the brakes as before the change was effected.

To release the pawl that holds the brake lever set, a small auxiliary pedal is necessary. This is made in the form of a bell-crank lever and pivoted on the pin at the bottom of the pedal lever. The back end of the lever is slotted to fit over a pin in the side of the pawl, and pressing the pedal forward throws the point of the pawl down and permits the brake lever to come forward. The auxiliary pedal is so shaped and mounted that it may be operated by the driver's heel. When the car is brought to a full stop, only the ball of the foot is used, and the pawl then locks the brake on.

When using the brake to slow down the car in conjunction with the service brake, the whole foot is used, and the pressure keeps the pawl from engaging, so that the brake pedal returns to the same position when the pressure was released.

A screen-door spring should be fitted to the brake lever as shown, so that it will be pulled forward as soon as the pawl is released.

— G. A. Luers, Washington, D.C.

(*Popular Mechanics*, March 1924)

Removing play in Ford fan

The new style Ford fans often develop end play due to excessive wear. As the front end of such fans is closed, the fan would have to be taken off and the blades removed from the pulley before the shaft could be turned in to remedy the play in the usual manner. A better way of taking up this play is to remove the cotter pin from the locknut at the rear end of the fan shaft and loosen the lock about one full turn. Then place a cotter pin through the nut and the fan shaft, but do not spread the ends of the cotter pin.

Next, turn the locknut with a wrench and the fan shaft will turn with it. Turn the shaft in until only a very slight end play can be felt. Then remove the cotter pin through the locknut and tighten it. Replace the cotter pin through the locknut and spread the ends. The locknut on such fans must be kept tight and the cotter pin in place, or the fan will eventually turn the shaft in so tightly that the fan will stop revolving.

(*Popular Mechanics*, November 1926)

Special Automotive Steels
Henry Ford

Vanadium, the new element, imparts qualities to steel which are little less than magical

If there has ever been any basis for the claim that foreign-made motor-cars were superior to the American product it has been the fact that until recently the American manufacturer was unable to obtain metals, particularly steels, that possessed the necessary qualities to fully meet his requirements.

America is by far the largest steel-producing country in the world, but the demands for ordinary commercial steels have been greater than the output and consequently our mills have not had the time nor felt the inclination to go into the special steel branch of the art save in a purely experimental way.

The requirements of the motor-car, with its enormous power in proportion to weight, the high speeds of which it is capable, and the severe stresses frame, axles, and other chassis parts are therefore called upon to withstand, have confounded the engineers and exhausted the profoundest lore of our metallurgists. A people who occupied the foremost position in the engineering world — the greatest builders of locomotives, of bridges, and machinery of all kinds — we still possessed little knowledge that was of value to us when confronted with the problems that arise in and are peculiar to the construction of the modern motor locomotive; and we had no steels that were adequate for our needs.

American methods of manufacture and American workmanship, both of the hand and the machine, are superior to those of older countries — many hoary superstitions and beliefs to the contrary notwithstanding. European makers are studying American methods and importing American automatic machinery as fast as they can get it — which, by the way, is not very rapidly, for never before was the demand for all kinds of machine tools so greatly in excess of the supply as at the present moment.

The question of supremacy in motor-car building, as between the American and foreign producer, resolved itself into a matter of materials. With proper steels at our command the "Yankee Peril" would become a reality, for not only will the tide of import subside, but we shall soon begin to make serious inroads on European trade.

The problem was not merely to obtain a steel that would carry a load or withstand the severest single strain or shock to which a car would be subjected in the life of the machine, but a metal of such toughness and tenacity as would successfully resist the ravages of vibration and fatigue. Fully eighty-five per cent of the stresses which the various parts of the automobile are called upon to withstand are of the kind known technically as "dynamic." In other branches of engineering a steel that would behave well when subjected to a steady load or a slowly applied bending action, and of sufficient ductility greatly before finally breaking under the load was sufficient for all requirements. When applied to automobile construction, however, it soon became apparent that ductility under such circumstances did not necessarily imply the certainty that the metal would behave well under stresses applied in a different manner; steel which showed great toughness and ductility under static loads was found to fracture like glass in some cases under the influence of shock or of constant vibration, such as that which we have to reckon with in an automobile.

Various alloys of nickel and chrome steels have been applied, and with varying degrees of success. Chrome adds toughness to steel when used in homeopathic quantities, but when used to the extent of more than about one per cent, its effectiveness on the steel is so injurious as to more than counteract the benefits derived from it. Nickel, while adding certain static qualities, is wholly devoid of dynamic qualities or virtues.

To quote the views of an eminent metallurgist, Mr. J. Kent Smith: "Heretofore the automobile engineer has contented himself with steels which possess the necessary static qualifications — in other words, about

continued on page 94

FORD "SOUND LOGIC" TALKS

QUANTITY PRODUCTION
MAKES HIGHER QUALITY POSSIBLE

1907

No. 1 GET THE SERIES

WE ARE NOW THE LARGEST producers of motor cars in the world, unquestionably. (Both in point of number of cars and in cash volume of business per annum.)

BUT THE QUESTION NATURALLY ARISES: "Must not quality be sacrificed in order to produce the quantities, and must not the low prices be made possible by the use of cheap materials, or work, or both?" Lots of successful men are unversed in the problems of manufacturing, though familiar with other kinds of wholesaling.

HERE'S INCONTESTABLE PROOF of our contention, "Ford cars are cheap only in price," and that quantity production not only does not necessitate sacrifice of quality, but actually enables us to put better materials, more accurate work in the making of a $600 car than has hitherto been practicable in American cars, even when sold at fancy prices—prices dictated not by quality, though that is the claim, but by antiquated methods and lack of facilities to do things the Ford way.

VANADIUM-CHROME STEEL is acknowledged by all metallurgists to possess qualities for meeting the conditions peculiar to motor car usage to an extent unobtainable in any other steel or alloy known. The price of this steel—due largely to the fact that it has been made only in small lots in crucibles or experimental furnaces of 2 to 4 tons—has made it a "commercial impossibility," as makers express it. Recently this special steel was brought a bit nearer by the discovery of a large deposit of vanadiferous ore. There was a race to get it. A certain engineers' association began to experiment—tried to corner the market.

AS USUAL FORD WAS FIRST. We didn't corner the market—didn't try to. But three weeks ago we made the first Vanadium steel ever made in 40-ton heats and by the open hearth process. Made several different grades each for a specific use, as springs, axles, crank-shafts, gears, connecting rods and frames. We are still the only American makers who use Vanadium steel in motor car construction.

AND FROM NOW ON Vanadium-chrome steel will be used throughout in all Ford models—runabouts as well as six-cylinder touring cars. Let others follow as soon as they can—we figure they're about a year and a half behind at present.

OUR DEMANDS FOR STEEL amount to 280 tons per month—four or five at least of our competitors would have to combine to make it possible for them to use Vanadium steel—and then the cost would make it necessary to charge you two prices for it.

BY THE WAY, we were the first and are still, so far as we know, the only makers who appreciate the wonderful results of scientific HEAT-TREATMENT OF STEEL PARTS AFTER FORGING OR PRESSING—the only concern in America who put every piece of steel through that "doubling-the-efficiency" process before machining. Ask about it—ten to one they won't know what you are talking about.

THAT FORD PRICES—Prices that stagger competition and leave a doubt even in the minds of buyers as to the possible value of the cars—are made possible by our methods of quantity production, is now conceded by those who know.

Ford 1907 Line

$2800

Six-cylinder Car
Touring or Runabout

$600

Famous Model "N"
Four-cylinder Runabout

$750

Model R, Four-cylinder
"Edition de Luxe"

PRICES F. O. B. DETROIT

FORD MOTOR COMPANY, FACTORY AND MAIN OFFICE, DETROIT, MICH.

BRANCH RETAIL STORES: New York, Philadelphia, Boston, Chicago, Buffalo, Cleveland, Detroit and Kansas City.

Canadian trade supplied by Ford Motor Company of Canada, Walkerville, Ont.

Ford talks: "Quantity production makes higher quality possible."

continued from page 92

fifteen per cent of his requirements—and having made sure of this small percentage he hoped that in some way he had obtained the other eighty-five per cent."

Recently a new element has entered the special steel making industry, and one which will revolutionize American metallurgy. I say American, but the term need not be so restricted, for while this element is known to a limited extent in Europe, especially in England, it is by no means universally known or—for that matter—used in construction of motor-cars there.

I speak of vanadium.

This mineral element, when judiciously used, imparts to steel qualities that are little less than magical, and which are well calculated to meet the most severe requirements of the automobile engineer.

The question naturally arises, why has not this valuable element been more widely known and used in the past? The answer is a simple one. Until within a few months the entire output of vanadium in the world has been about two hundred pounds per month. This had to be extracted by a very expensive process, and even then the supply, limited as it was to two or three sources, was sufficient only to give it an academic value. In other words, while most metallurgists knew of the existence of vanadium, and were to some extent aware of its value in steel-making, where dynamic qualities were desirable, it occupied a place similar to that of a more recently discovered element—radium. We knew its wonder-working qualities, but its price of one million dollars per pound or so renders this knowledge of little practical value to us.

Fortunately for the automobile industry, and still more fortunately for the automobile user of the future, a large source of supply of this valuable material has been recently opened up, and vanadium in commercial quantities is now available to the American steelmaker. During the past few weeks exhaustive tests and experiments with vanadium-chrome steels have been made at the United States proving-grounds, both in armor-plate and projectile forms; and no less interesting tests for several months past have been carried on by automobile engineers, with the net result that vanadium steel has proven to be the metal *par excellence* for automobile construction.

Unlike nickel, chrome, manganese, and other mineral elements that are used in special steelmaking, vanadium contains within itself no virtues; but in its action on the other elements it confers upon the steel almost miraculous properties—for be it said the most successful application of vanadium lies in the direction of quaternary steels, such as chromium or nickel-vanadium steels. In order to obtain the best results with these elements it is necessary to add the vanadium in small doses and with proper precautions, as vanadium is a very powerful medicine and possesses to a marked degree the property of "elusiveness." To use a simple term, it acts as a physic on the other elements, and in a technical sense retards the segregation of the carbides, and thereby produces a steel of very fine texture and of great uniformity, as are clearly shown under the microscope.

For service in automobile axles, frames, gears, engine crank-shafts, and driving shafts, vanadium-chrome steels have been shown to be superior to anything else ever produced for this particular service. Of course the particular alloy which is most suitable for frames is not equally suitable for crank-shafts or for gears. But various grades of vanadium steels—various alloys possessing the different qualities to meet the different kinds of service—are now produced on a commercial basis in America. One of the advantages of vanadium is that its use permits the application of a larger percentage of chromium than would otherwise be permissible for the reasons previously outlined. In short, without going more exhaustively into the matter, it may be said that by the introduction of this new element in steel-making the strength of an automobile axle may be doubled without causing an increase in the dimensions or weight, and the working capacity and shock-resisting qualities of that member in actual usage multiplied many times.

Just to what extent vanadium will prove valuable in brass, aluminum, iron castings and other metals used in motor-car construction has not yet been fully determined, but many eminent scientists are now at work on these problems, and the results so far have been most gratifying.

Fortunately for automobile manufacturers and users the industry has attained to such proportions that its demands now merit the attention of steel-makers, and vanadium, having come within commercial reach, nothing is left to be desired in the way of materials to meet the severest requirements of the engineer. This, combined with American methods and workmanship, will produce automobiles of a quality unsurpassed in any particular by cars made in Europe—a claim that in all sincerity and candor we have not hitherto been able to make.

(*Harper's Weekly*, March 16, 1907.)

Chapter 7

Fittings for the Ford

Changes that are no improvement and others that are advisable

From J.L. Edmiston, California. — In a recent issue a correspondent makes inquiry as to the value of the multitude of accessories and fittings specially designed for the Model T Ford. Occasionally one of your correspondents advances the idea that the makers of the car must know just what is best for his product and that

therefore it must be assumed that he has supplied it with every useful and desirable feature, and that the

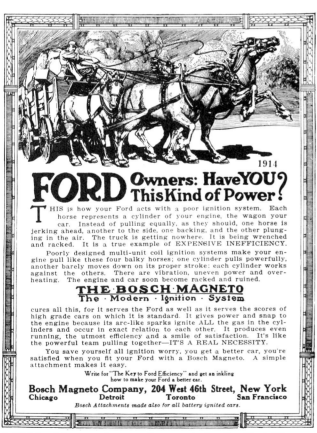

A 1914 ad for a replacement magneto for the Model T.

A 1914 ad for a "master vibrator" offered as a superior replacement for the box of four standard vibrators on the Model T. Advantages are enumerated clearly in the ad.

FYRAC
Spark PLUGS

One INCH firing surface (PATENTED)

instead of

one firing POINT

A 7,000 mile Ford test

Another dramatic test of Fyrac performance! A grilling that covered 7,073 miles in 14 states and two Canadian provinces—through nine mountain ranges and 17 days of rain. This is the test that Joseph C. Hubner, Hamilton, Ohio, gave Fyrac Spark Plugs in his Ford car. He ran for hours in low gear, and one climb of 31 miles was made almost entirely in low. All these obstacles were met unflinchingly by Fyrac. "The plugs were never touched," says Mr. Hubner.

After the trip, out of curiosity, Mr. Hubner removed the spark plug from cylinder No. 1. "No. 1 is the cylinder that usually gives trouble in Ford cars," says Mr. Hubner; "but we found the firing wires of the Fyrac in perfect condition—only a slight amount of carbon on the side walls and none on the firing surface."

In *your* car, regardless of make, you will get from Fyrac the same kind of dependable service as Mr. Hubner. Fyrac's one INCH firing surface—with its 7 to 10 sparks to every explosion—means more power, greater gas mileage and less gasoline-formed carbon. Ask your dealer about Fyrac Plugs. Fyrac Manufacturing Company, Rockford, Illinois.

Yellow Cabs of Chicago and New York, the former the world's largest taxicab system, use Fyrac Spark Plugs.

$1 for Your OLD Spark Plugs

Take your old set of spark plugs, no matter what their make or condition, to your Fyrac dealer. He will allow you ONE DOLLAR for them on a new set of Fyracs. Get rid of your old plugs at a profit! "Fyrac" your motor—give it the benefit of one INCH firing surface in every cylinder. Do it while this offer is in force!

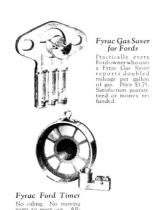

Fyrac Gas Saver for Fords
Practically every Ford owner who uses a Fyrac Gas Saver reports doubled mileage per gallon of gas. Price $3.75. Satisfaction guaranteed or money refunded.

Fyrac Ford Timer
No oiling. No moving parts to wear out. All-metal track insures even wear. Brush keeps track clean, insuring a smooth-running motor. Will last longer than ordinary timers. Price $2.00.

A 1923 spark plug ad featuring a plug with an unusual sparking arrangement—with "one inch firing surface," giving "7 to 10 sparks to every explosion." While many of these multiple-firing plugs have appeared on the market, none of them have survived.

owners are but inviting trouble by making changes or additions, whatsoever.

This position, to my mind, is about as logical as would be the contention that the Ford comes supplied with a pair of pliers and a wrench or two, so the purchase of additional tools is but folly on the part of the owner wishing to make his own adjustments and replacements. It is true the Ford comes regularly equipped with all that is absolutely necessary to its successful operation. Of this there can be no question, since they are supplying a jack with the 1913 cars. It is, however, equally true, that a few additions to the regular equipment will add greatly to the convenience of the operator and even contribute to the increased efficiency of the car. An intelligent discretion, however, should always be used, and it is not necessary to accept at face value all the roseate representations of accessory salesmen and part makers.

As an example of how not to do it, I may mention an instance which came to my attention recently where the owner had at considerable expense discarded the magneto for ignition and installed a widely advertised battery system. Efficient to be sure, but not one whit better than the factory system, and with the added expense of keeping a bunch of a dozen dry cells at working voltage.

He put on a Presto tank—better than the generator of course, but surely "carrying coals to Newcastle," when placed on the Ford car with its electric possibilities. Then a device guaranteed to keep the water in the cooling system in perpetual motion, which may have done no harm, but which is quite uncalled for, as with proper care and handling the Ford will run all day and never boil the water. As a fitting finish to the collection he had his side lamps wired to run from the magneto!

In the light of my experiences there are just four changes I should make at once on buying a new Ford car. These would be an oil gauge for the transmission case, a muffler cut-out, a device for supplying auxiliary air to the intake manifold, and I would have the car wired to run electric head-lights from the magneto. To this list some would add a master vibrator, and in-

The Watchman On Your Dash

Eliminates the possibility of burned-out bearings and scored cylinders. It warns you when the oil is not circulating, or when the oil level is low.

In addition, the ZIM DASH OIL FEED is a positive, independent forced feed lubricating system.

The ZIM DASH OIL FEED reduces repairs. It saves time and the nuisance of under-the-car inspection. It saves fuel, by insuring proper lubrication always.

Adapted to every style of Ford car. Two types: For Dash or Instrument Board Installation.

Dealers are making money out of the ZIM DASH OIL FEED. They are also making satisfied customers.

Write for the Zim proposition.

ZIM ACCESSORIES CO., Room F, 208 N. Wabash Avenue, Chicago, Ill.

ZIM Dash Sight-Feed Oil System for Fords

As the writer pointed out, an oil gauge should certainly have been incorporated on all Fords from the beginning. No engine instrument is more important. This is from 1920.

Reproduced here is the only ad for a cut-out found for this period, 1928. Note the slightly exaggerated statement that "Leading cars have by-pass mufflers standard." Cutting out a muffler is, in fact, illegal, at least today, and this may account for the dearth of such ads, even in 1928.

A 1925 ad for an "automatic carburetion" device for the Model T. Many such devices appeared but none of them have survived.

deed a number of the 1913 cars are coming from the factory so equipped. Properly adjusted, the ordinary coil will do the work and if none but the best quality spark plugs are used, the motor will run as smoothly and sweetly as one could ask for.

The matter of the spark plugs is of some importance and especially so if trouble is experienced in securing even adjustment of the vibrators, for the reason that a good plug will give an adequate spark and hence the perfect ignition requisite for a smooth running engine over a wider range of more or less imperfect vibrator adjustment than will a plug of indifferent quality.

In the matter of the oil gauge on the transmission case, its cost is so trivial and its convenience – I might almost say its necessity – so obvious, that why the factory does not include it in the regular equipment is one of the things seemingly past finding out. Depending on the petcocks, the operator has no means of knowing with certainty if he has oil for five miles or fifty miles unless he either fills the case to the level of the upper one, or drains the oil down to the lower level and then puts in a stated quantity. With the gauge attached, the glass shows at a glance the exact level of the oil in the case, and the disappearance of the oil on starting the motor is proof the reading is correct.

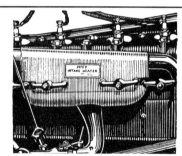

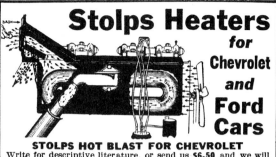
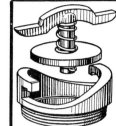

Apco Shock Absorber ad.

The cut-out, while hardly to be classified as a necessity, is still a desired feature, enabling the operator to determine readily just how hard his motor is laboring under the load, and is also a convenience when correcting ignition troubles as well as giving trifle more power and allowing the motor to run slightly cooler on a hard pull. The utility of the third item on my list is perhaps not so generally understood and recognized as in the case with the oil gauge and cut-out, and a car chiefly for use on city streets—short runs and frequent stops—there is little to be gained by having it installed unless hills are to be considered. On a continuous run, however, a suitable device for admitting air into the manifold above the carburetor makes possible a pronounced economy in gasoline consumption as the mixture can be instantly and perfectly adjusted to suit varying conditions of load and engine speed.

In addition to its value as a fuel saver, the device is also a great convenience in a hilly country, as in descending a hill, the mere opening of the air valve, immediately stops ignition, causing the car to run against the engine compression (the clutch being engaged) and materially saving wear and tear on the brakes. This also saves gasoline, as with the valve

Detroit Steering Control—"can be installed in forty minutes."

wide open and throttle closed, no gas is drawn through the carburetor.

There are several contrivances for the purposes on the market, differing in detail but no doubt giving substantially similar results. Whatever pattern is selected, however, should have the control lever on the steering post. On my own car I have the "Saunders" and a friend recently put the same on his 1912 car which he had run

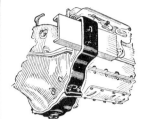

Motor mount stabilizer ad.

Hassler Shock Absorber ad.

Milwaukee Timer "flattens hills" with proper ignition timing.

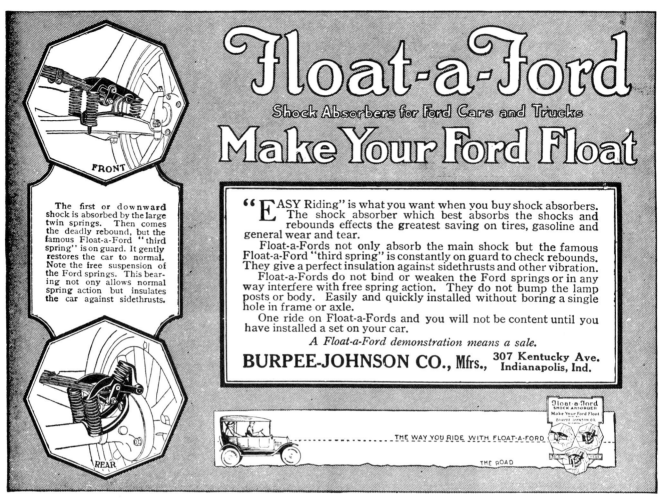
about eight thousand miles, previously averaging less than twenty miles to the gallon. Next day after installing the air valve he made the one hundred and forty mile run to San Diego on four and a half gallons of gasoline, being better than thirty-one miles to the gallon. This is an extreme case, no doubt, as he may have been using an unnecessarily rich mixture before, but it illustrates the facility with which the mixture can be adjusted for best results.

The matter of electric lights vs. gas is more a question of individual preference. I prefer the electric system as being more economical, as well as more convenient, and gives a better light than gas except at slow engine speeds.

(*Automobile Dealer and Repairer*, February 1913. The above article was written by a Model T owner and shows the early concern for Model T improvements.)

Ford's rebuttal: "The most perfect machine"

The above Model T owner's comments regarding needed improvements in the Model T can be con-trasted with the following statements of the Ford Motor Company, regarding the need for any improvements in their products, taken from some early newspaper advertisements:

A 1903 ad, for instance, stated "This new (Model A) light touring car . . . is positively the most perfect machine on the market, having overcome all obstacles such as smell, noise, jolts, etc., common to all other makes of Auto Carriages." The model referred to was described as the Fordmobile, with detached tonneau.

In a 1925 ad headed "Ford, Today's High Peak in Motor Value," readers of *The American Motorist* learned that "Many other important changes and improvements characterize the Ford improved open and closed cars. The fact that all this has been accomplished without raise in prices is even more impressive than the changes themselves. Ford value, for years holding unchallenged leadership in the motor car field, now reaches a new peak through the volume and economy of Ford manufacture."

Make Your Ford an Easy Rider

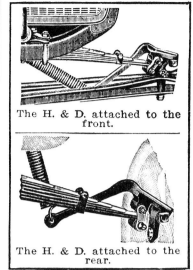

The H. & D. attached to the front.

The H. & D. attached to the rear.

Genuine H. & D. Shock Absorbers $3.95

Here is the big shock absorber hit of the season for Ford owners. Moreover, we offer it at a price that seems almost impossible. Ford owners everywhere are intensely interested in this simple but perfect little shock absorber; are trying it out and immediately giving it their hearty endorsement. They can't say enough for it after having ridden in a car equipped with it. It responds instantly to the slightest jar and checks the hardest jolts so effectively that you do not realize you have bumped over anything. Consider what such a shock eliminator means to the mechanism of your car. Then consider the price. Note the simplicity. No complicated parts and nothing to get out of order. Special care has been taken to make all parts that receive any strain extra strong. In fact, we guarantee this absorber to not only please you, but we guarantee it against breakage for the life of your car. Quickly attached. No holes to bore and everything furnished complete. Made of malleable iron. Illustrations show how absorber is attached front and rear. Set consists of four, two for front and two for rear. Shipping weight, 20 pounds.

161R4879—For Touring Model. Price set................**$3.95**
161R4880—For Roadster Model. Price, set...............

Easy Rider Touring and Roadster shocks.

Chapter 8

High-Performance and Racing Accessories

Shows you how easy it is to convert your Ford
Model T into a fast, saucy, sports car—designed
on airplane speed principles!

Certainly no one ever considered the Model T as the basis for a racer. Its leisurely gait belied that possibility, although it is said to have been speedy compared to the competition, with its four-cylinder, 20 hp engine; or was it because of a lack of speed that some adventuresome souls tried to instill a little more life into the Model T with special equipment and even streamlined bodies?

Rajo's 1921 ad for their overhead-valve unit. It is obviously a professional-looking job, which probably explains why the price was not quoted.

Still, there were oodles of other makes on the road that were as slow, so that can't be the reason for efforts to make the Model T go faster. The reasons seem to have been its wide availability, low price or its apparently indestructible nature, especially of its engine. This was due to the fact that the engine was so lightly stressed, with a compression ratio of 4:1 or less. Combined with ample construction, the sturdy engine could withstand considerable hopping-up without getting temperamental, throwing a rod or burning out a piston. As for breathing ability, while others later offered larger valves, the factory always listed the engine's valves as "extra large."

The great majority of hop-up items, however, were not concerned with major changes in the engine. Only a few firms offered properly designed and effective parts to replace such things as the head or the cast-iron pistons ("the finest grey iron"). Crankshafts, con rods and camshafts were of vanadium steel and could not be improved. Aluminum pistons were, of course, offered by others; these, combined with the overhead-valve arrangement, improved engine speed and output. The outstanding example of this can be seen in the Fronty head, which increased the standard T output from 20 hp to 80 hp.

Most overhead-valve heads had a single camshaft operating the usual two valves per cylinder. Only one twin-cam head has been observed in commercial ads for Model Ts, this being the one offered by Laurel Motors of Anderson, Indiana. Their "Roof 16 overhead valve equipment" produced, according to their 1919 ad, "One hundred percent extra efficiency, with greater gasoline and oil economy for either touring car or truck. Hill climbing for the touring car owner beyond his wildest dreams. . . . Ford cars with our 16-valve equipment have been rivals of the best racing cars on mile and a half tracks and have practically driven the high priced racing cars from competition."

While Laurel advertised both a single- and a double-overhead-cam head, their double-overhead-cam head merely operated the conventional two valves per cylinder.

Rajo promised, in their 1924 ads, that their Model B valve-in-head transplant "provides its owners with the most powerful car on the road." A vehicle so equipped, the ad continued, "will jump to 50 miles per hour in two city blocks!"

Most performance-boosting items consisted of more prosaic items, primarily carburetors, pistons, rings and even spark plugs, though some more sophisticated offerings consisted of substituting a three- or four-speed transmission for the planetary two-speed epicyclic standard unit. This seems to have been a favorite of Henry Ford's. He even planned on continuing its use in the Model A but was ultimately persuaded by Edsel Ford to abandon it.

Ads offering to furnish racy bodies, not to be confused with racing bodies, for the Model T abounded in the twenties, especially in *Popular Mechanics* and *Popular Science* magazines. The golden age for home-built Model T bodies was from 1922 to 27. One ad from The Central Auto Supply Company of Louisville, Kentucky, began under an attractive example of their product. "Save exorbitant freight rates and one-half original cost by buying Ford Speedster Bodies knocked-down. Simple, complete instructions furnished, all parts cut to exact fit. Anyone can assemble this job. Complete with hood, radiator shell, instrument board, upholstering, metal parts, wood parts, bolts, screws, etc. Flat radiator shell furnished made up. Designed low with lack of wind resistance. Price set up $90.00, further particulars on request."

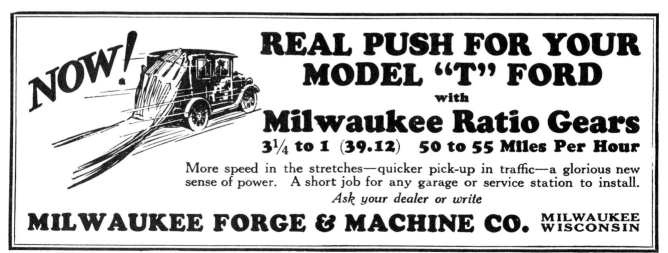
A 1928 ad for "speed gear" for the Model T. This produced a top speed of 55 mph, up from approximately 37 mph.

An article devoted to these variations was printed in *Motor World* for February 12, 1914, under the heading, "Small Touring Machine Can be Closed Car, Too."

"Small cars have increased and multiplied with such rapidity that it is by no means surprising that among the multitude of users, there should be many who want to use their machines in all kinds of weather and in all seasons," the article began. "It is for these year-round users that several styles of detachable or convertible bodies have been designed. . . .

"The Mandel 'limosette' which is built by the Mandel Limousine Co. . . . is designed especially for Ford cars and is a separate unit that is put on the regular Ford touring body and will fit all cars of the 1912, 1913 and 1914 models. It is of composite construction, of steel and wood, with brass trimmings, mahogany ceiling and window framing, and broadcloth upholstery. The windows can be opened and the doors connect with the permanent doors so that both open together.

"Of the forward doors, only one, that on the driver's right, is made to open. A windshield is incorporated with the structure, and over it the hood projects in an overhang that not only adds much to the appearance, but also serves as an additional protection in inclement weather. Where the front of the body joins the dashboard there is a rounded steel cowl that makes an extremely neat finish. In fact, the appearance of the 'Limosette' leaves little to be desired, and the makers say that it is absolutely weatherproof and also extremely durable.

"The body can be attached to a Ford car without other preparation than the removal of the standard top and windshield. No tools are required except an ordinary monkey-wrench and the only assistance needed is for the lifting on and the balancing of the body — which, incidentally, weighs but 150 pounds. A smaller type is made to fit Ford roadsters and costs $100. The general construction is the same in both cases."

Mandel also offered a new body for the Ford Roadster. Under a photo of their Roadster body, which

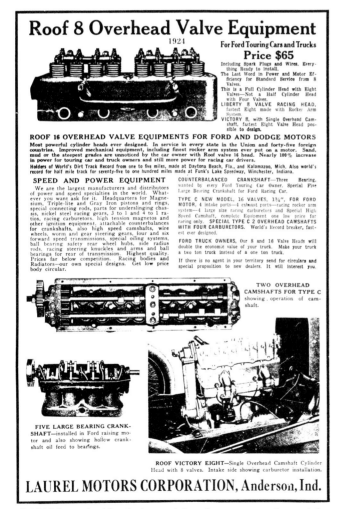

A 1919 Laurel ad for their special performance equipment, including a sixteen-valve overhead-valve cylinder head.

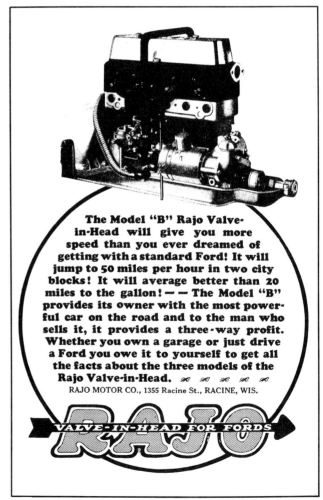

A 1924 Rajo ad for their Model B "valve-in-head" unit which produced better gas mileage as well as top speed.

A 1922 ad for a four-speed transmission for the Model T. Several similar units were offered during the twenties.

This 1919 ad offered the Arrow Racing Body, one of the better-looking bodies available. Note the continued price escalation. Even fenders were $15 extra. Several factory colors were offered, as well as blue.

looked reasonably attractive and was available for $100, f.o.b. Chicago, the copy read, "In design and construction, the Mandel Limosette for Ford Roadsters is the same as for the touring car. The Roadster Limosette is invaluable for professional and business men who must ride their cars in all kinds of weather.

It gives all the comforts and pleasures of the closed car at less than one-half the regular cost. The Roadster Limosette can be attached in about thirty minutes. When attached it adds but 40 lbs. to the weight of the

Model T Speedsters and Sportsters

Numerous ads appeared during the twenties, offering "sporting" or "speedster" bodies ready to be bolted or glued to your prosaic Model T. They might not have made your car faster, even with streamlining, but, boy oh boy, were they ever the cat's patootie! It was the era of "Oh you kid!" and "Twenty-three skidoo!" Your granddad, or even your great-granddad was the Sheik and his girlfriend was his Sheba, as they drove by in their Torpedo Speedster, still sounding, however, just like a Model T.

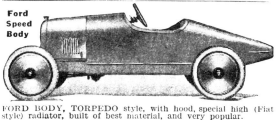

Ford Roadster. The Limosette makes the Ford double serviceable. Attach it in Winter—detach it in Summer."

The Convertible Automobile Body Corporation of New York City offered about the same time the Lewkowicz Convertible Body, for which patents had been applied. Copy resembling that of Mandel's stated

that this was also "Two bodies in one—a touring body when you want it—a closed car when you need it. The change is made in less than one minute!"

The ad continued with these modest words: "The Lewkowicz Convertible Body is a wonder of mechanical construction. No tools necessary! Not a screw! not

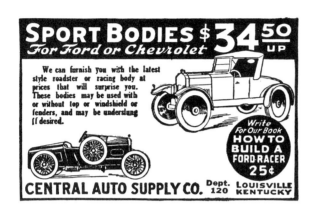

a bolt! not a pin! is used in making the change in either direction. So easy that even the most delicate woman can do it! The windows drop in their casing on the side of the car, like in the most expensive Limousine. Waterproof! airproof! coldproof! Solid and staunch as a Limousine. When touring anywhere—and you are caught in a storm—without even soiling your hands you can get full protection in less than thirty seconds!

"Ford owners—You are the majority of owners in the United States. We have designed the automobile for you shown in the pictures—to fit Ford Cars Model 'T.' Ford dealers and agents—Double your income by handling the Lewkowicz Convertible Body. Apply immediately for territorial rights."

The mid-teens ad for the above Greyhound Speedster body contained the following copy: "This body is

Be Your Own Top Maker

WE manufacture a complete line of auto fabrics for Ford and all other makes of automobiles. All materials ready to put on. Complete instructions with every purchase.

Schneider's DeLuxe One-Man Top, complete with side curtains for Ford **$32.50**

Our Ford Top Recovering No. 10—Pantasote guaranteed, which includes two nickel-plated bevel glass windows.......... **$12.50**

Our Ford Top Recovering No. 6— Includes two glass windows.......... **$6.95**

Back Curtain with 2 Glass Windows, $2.50
Slip Covers from $4.50 up

Send for Samples of Materials and Catalogue No. 3

DEALERS WRITE FOR SPECIAL PROPOSITION

A. E. SCHNEIDER MFG. CO.

4265 Hudson Blvd.   WEST HOBOKEN, N. J.

SLEEP IN YOUR FORD!

Camp out in any weather—save hotel bills. Two can sleep comfortably in this Folding Ford Bed. Ready for use in 4 minutes—doesn't injure Ford. Sedan or touring car models —$14.50.

SEND NO MONEY

Live Sales Opportunities. just pay postman. Money back guarantee. Order from
Write or wire.
OUTERS EQUIPMENT CO., 820 Mayer Bldg., Milwaukee, Wis.

Make Your Ford a Closed Car!

Limo weather-proof sections will change your 1923-1924 Ford Touring or Roadster, into classy limousine-style closed car. Doors open from outside. Sliding front panels for ventilation. Three-ply, double covered veneer frames. Color matches your top. Easily, quickly installed. Guaranteed. Low priced. Fine for bad weather. *Write for prices.*
BUOB & SCHEU, Dept. A-8, 216 Webster St., Cincinnati, O.

"THE BROADWAY"

The K-37 is the classiest sport body for Fords in America. Built of 20 Gauge Lead-Coated Steel, upholstered in very high grade black or Spanish brown material. Spring Cushions. Stylish one-man top with side curtains. Door on right side of body with inside nickel lever. 12-gallon gas tank. Adjustable plate glass windshield. *Send for Descriptive Circular and Price List.*
Champion Racingbody Co., Dept. P.M., 7-9 E. 28th St., Chicago, Ill.

SEND for the INTERNATIONAL CATALOG

FOR FORD—PRICES FROM $27.85 UP.
Factory to Consumer direct—Pay only one profit.

Our net price list. Full line of auto bodies and accessories for Fords at Wholesale Prices.
Save big money on bodies by buying direct from factory.

INTERNATIONAL BODY WORKS, Dept. 7, 914 W. Ohio Street, CHICAGO, ILL.

You Can Save $50.00

By recovering your old auto top frame yourself. We make these recovers to fit all makes and models of cars. Any person that can drive a car can put it on. We furnish instructions. Roof and quarters sewed together $7.65 and up Parcels Post Paid with rear curtain, fasteners, welts and tacks. All complete. Give us the name, year and model number of your car, and we will send you our catalogue with samples and quote you exact price.

LIBERTY TOP & TIRE CO., Dept. E7, Cincinnati, O.

"LYON" WINTER TOPS

ROADSTER **$31**²⁵
TOURING $41.25
FOR
FORD and CHEVROLETS

Late models. Warm, roomy and comfortable. Easily ventilated when desired. Don't envy others. Be comfortable yourself. *Send for our "Special Fall Bulletin" containing also our full line of racing bodies.*
AUTO TIRE SALES CO., Dept. P15
1346 S. Michigan Ave.   CHICAGO   Body Division

specially designed to be lighter and stronger than other racing bodies and at the same time to be symmetrical and pleasing to the eye. It will relieve your Ford of a great deal of weight and increase the power and speed of your engine. You will immediately notice the difference. The car will take up speed smoothly and quickly without the usual jerking motion and will fairly sail through the air because of its particular non-friction shape.

"It can be quickly attached to any Ford chassis. Frame work is the finest selected, kiln-dried hard

An outstanding example of a homebuilt racing body on a 1920 Model T chassis. Seen several years ago at a Model T get-together at Catalina, California.

wood. Cowl dash is correctly designed and the bucket seats are fitted with removable upholstering.

"Note the graceful and well-balanced placement of the 18-gallon oval gas tank with the 5-gallon round Polarine tank immediately behind it. Tanks have direct connections with the motor. Tool box is built in the body; fenders are long racy design. A speedster body that is unsurpassed.

"Width of body, 32 inches; length of body, 83 inches; length over all, 11½ feet. Seats 16x18 inches. All screw construction. Tanks, tank supports, seats, tool box and cowl are pressed steel with heavy rolled wire edge. Trimming of seats and cushions a clear, lustrous red with black edge binding and diamond quilted backs.

"Note—radiator, engine hood and lamps not included with outfit. Painted Battleship Gray, Light Blue with white stripe, or Red with black stripe."

The Sypher Manufacturing Company of Toledo, Ohio, got down to business in a few sentences in their one-inch ads. Under the heading "Oh Boy! 25 Miles Per Hour," the magazine reader was informed that 25 mph "is record of our stock car, using our special 1922 motor. Anyone can assemble this car. Send 30 cents for plans, instructions and price list of parts." Illustrating the ad was a youth waving to readers as he enthusiastically drove along in his Sypher Special.

The Victor Auto Body Company of Chicago was equally sparing in copy in its ads. Under the heading, "The Dragon," referring to the standard racing type of body illustrating the ad, was another youth waving at the reader as he zoomed along in a Dragon, a fairly conventional racing-type vehicle of the period. The few lines of copy in the ad read, "A special body for Fords. Comes complete with aluminum shell. We also manufacture other beautiful models. Live distributors wanted. Make big money handling Victor bodies for Fords. Write for catalog."

A 1925 ad included a testimonial from a satisfied customer. Regarding his purchase of material for Kuempel's Pal model, the satisfied customer wrote, "Total material cost with steel and paint for my Pal only $14.31. It took me just three Sundays to build it and I am sure proud to hear them say 'He's built that snappy sport car.' I never cut any steel or did any woodwork before but one can't go wrong with Kuempel patterns. (Signed) Wilfred Eno, Overland City, St. Louis, Mo."

The Kuempel Company of Guttenberg, Iowa, was one of the earliest advertisers of special bodies for the Model T. In 1918, they ran an ad entitled "Build This Speedster Yourself for only $4." The ad was illustrated with a fairly attractive speedster, which, unfortunately, is not of sufficiently good quality to reproduce. The copy included "With the remarkably simple

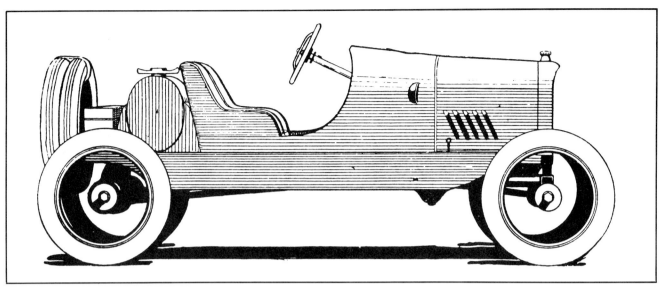

The above drawing and following copy appeared in a national mail-order catalog, circa 1925. The heading read, "Make a Full-Fledged Speedster of your Ford." Under the subhead "Cyclone Speedster Body," the copy read, "Here is a real nifty speedster body that would do credit to any car. We have cor-rectly named it Cyclone because it glides so easily, noise-lessly through the air on any Model T Ford chassis. A body of this design lightens the burden on the engine and means more speed. Just about the best value available to the Beau Brummel of 1925."

sure-fit, Red-I-Cut system of patterns, you can make your FordCar into one of the classiest speedsters on the road, with all the appearance of a $1500 car—in a few hours! Anyone can do it with Red-I-Cut patterns, a saw, hammer, screw driver and materials bought at any hardware store. The bodies stand low, keep the road, hug the turns at all speeds, weigh less, saving tires, gas and oil, have livelier pick up, greater riding comfort—designed on airplane speed principles."

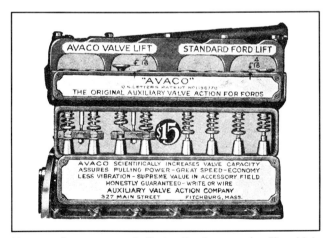

Here can be seen an ad offering the Avaco valve lift, which, according to the ad, raised valve travel from ⁴/₁₆ to ⁷/₁₆ in., as-suring better pulling power, greater speed, more economy, greater value and less vibration with the Model T engine. This sounds reasonable, as greater valve travel should have resulted in better cylinder breathing. All for $15—1926 dol-lars, that is.

Many well-established firms offered Model T replacement parts, including Stromberg, Gray & Davis, and Bosch. Here is a 1917 ad for Hammered rings for the Model T.

111

L.L. Corum in his 1923 Model T Speedster which placed fifth in the Indy 500 that year. Indianapolis Motor Speedway

The Kuempel Company was prolific during the twenties as well. Another ad was headlined, "Make Your FORD Into The ACE." The illustration showed a rather racy sort of fastback model—at least racy for 1923. Copy began with, "Get ready for spring—Build your Ace now." For only $5.99 one could get a Red-i-Kut life-size set of patterns, as well as "picture illustrations [which] show you how easy it is to convert your Ford into this fast, saucy, sport car—as thousands have done with easily obtained materials. No need to lay up the car. Makes wonderful 4-passenger car." For only ten cents (coin) a reader could obtain an actual photo

of the Ace and a manual of distinctive sport car patterns, which started at $3.80. Also available were " 'RKO' Steel 'Swing Low' irons, tops, windshields, and many speed accessories."

Racetrack Model Ts

Lest the previous material give the reader the impression that the Model T was just a make-believe racer, let it be said that many participated in actual racing events. To everyone's surprise, driver L. L. Corum, shown seated in his T Speedster hopped up with a "Fronty" head, finished fifth in the 1923 Indy 500. The special head, developed in cooperation with Louis Chevrolet, produced 80 hp at 3600 rpm from the 121 cubic inch engine. He finished with only one pit stop and averaged just under 100 mph.

A year earlier, Glen Schultz of Colorado Springs, Colorado, won the Pikes Peak run in a Model T. Local newspapers reported the event as follows: "The recent Pikes Peak hill climb was a severe test on both cars and drivers for the 14-mile climb up a mountain road that rises one foot in every ten is surely no 'snap' for any car.

"Glen Schultz built up a special Ford car, and while the 'big car' drivers smiled at his entry, they soon realized their mistake, that the speed developed by this little car, was so much greater than the speed of their own machines that their efforts were useless.

Glen Schultz in his special hillclimbing Model T that won the 1922 Pikes Peak Run.

112

Described as a cutdown version of the 1919 Model T, the above racing body was offered the public with the following information: "The driver's seat is seven inches forward of the seat for the passenger, thus giving more elbow room. The seats are thirteen inches lower than the regular Ford seats.

The body drops eight inches below the frame. The outside exhaust is a feature liked by some of the drivers of the Speedster." Without a doubt the most professional looking and most beautiful body ever offered Model T owners for conversion.

"From the 'bang' of the starter's gun straight to the finish, the Ford 'showed them up' and at the end of the climb it finished 54 seconds ahead of its nearest rival."

A 1919 Laurel Motors ad featuring two Model T racers fitted with their four-valves-per-cylinder heads. These vehicles are reputed to have been able to do 100 mph.

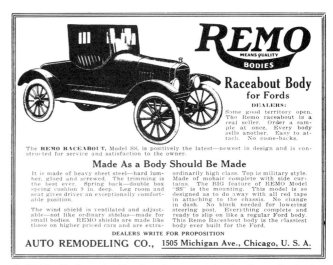
A 1919 offering of a Ford replacement body. Note the inclusion of "side curtains."

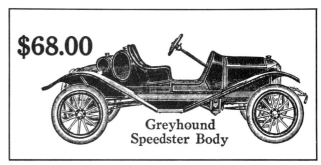
A mid-twenties speedster body which appears to have been usable as a racer, with the proper engine modifications.

The Ford Motor Company itself not only condoned racing with the Model T but participated officially in many such events. As early as 1909, Ford entered such events, not to break track records but rather production records, via the publicity generated by such events. That year, he entered two Model Ts in the Alaska-Yukon-Pacific Exposition's cross-continent race. It was to take place from New York and end in Seattle.

While thirty-five entries were received prior to the start of the race, only six entries actually showed up for the race. These were the two Model Ts with their 20 hp engines, a 48 hp Acme, a 45 hp Shawmut, a 50 hp Itala and an unspecified Stearns, probably the most powerful contender. Before the race, Ford had offered a public challenge to the others to beat his models. They could make their own terms. No offers were received.

The event was to be 4,106 miles long, with less than ten percent being "improved" roads. The first to drop out was the powerful Stearns, which lasted only twenty-four miles. The Model T number two was the first to arrive in Seattle, twenty-two days and fifty-five

This 1916 ad for alternate bodies was one of the few encountered that didn't show its product. As with many others, the pitch was also directed to dealers—in this case, primarily.

A 1919 ad for a graceful body replacement for the standard Model T.

A 1922 ad giving the potential Model T replacement prospect a choice of three different ways to go, with the first two offerings appearing rather attractive for the period.

114

Another mid-twenties or earlier racy replacement for the factory T body. Its specialty was the inclusion of cutout parts, "not paper patterns."

A 1922 ad offering a replacement body quite similar to that seen in the Central Auto Supply Company ad. Patterns were available for as little as $3.50. Note the "Pressed Metal Streamline Rear" available for $6.40 delivered."

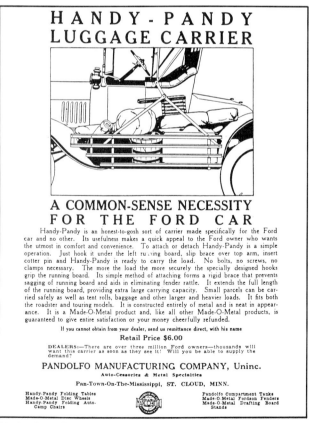
No body variation here, except in that the standard Model T body was modified with a "Handy-Pandy" luggage carrier offered in 1920.

minutes after leaving New York City. Second to arrive was the Shawmut, seventeen hours later. The Acme arrived six days later, while the Itala arrived by train, having conked out in Cheyenne, Wyoming. Ford number two, having become lost several times, was the last to arrive. It did so under its own power, however.

A 1919 ad offering a means of protecting your Model T's side curtains, via the patented, "No-Fault Pocket." Note that "All adjustments of curtains made from the seat without leaving the car."

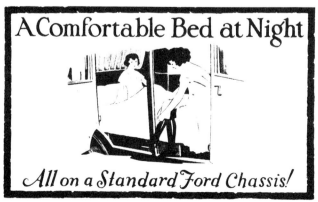

Another 1925 raceabout body offering for your Model T, with "Special Equipment," presumably engine modifications, for the serious T owner.

Even seat cover offerings weren't overlooked, as this 1924 ad indicates.

A recent ad for Model T restoration service and parts.

Ford was pleased with the publicity generated by his win, although some newspapers lambasted him and the race in general for the "dangerous, foolhardy, daredeviltrous clip of 40 to 50 miles per hour" speed of the competing vehicles. Ford himself took advantage of the situation by publishing a booklet on the subject entitled, "The Story of the Race," and distributing it to Ford dealers, simultaneously running ads in newspapers announcing that the race's winning car could be ordered from any Ford dealer.

The next year, Frank Kulick, driver of the winning car, challenged an ice boat across Lake St. Clair—and won, in the same car. He then went on to dirt track races in the East, where he won three firsts at Brighton Beach, following this up with victories at Syracuse.

In 1911, Ford racing victories continued, with five firsts and two seconds in New Orleans, against more powerful competitors. Then Kulick set a record at the Algonquin Hill Climb in Chicago. After that, in Mil-

A 1915 ad making a pitch for Model T dealers to handle a "Superior Stream-Line Hood."

This 1922 ad offered replacement parts at discount prices, as well as "Bodies for Ford cars."

waukee, he set records with three wins in two days. At the Detroit Fairgrounds, he won two preliminary events in his stripped-down Model T.

Kulick then switched to what was called his Super T variation, outwardly distinguished from production models only by its new, angled radiator. Inwardly, however, it contained a much more powerful engine, said only to have in common with the production Model T engine "its number of cylinders."

In his Super T, Kulick challenged Bob Burman driving his Blitzen Benz. With Henry Ford himself on hand to watch the results, Kulick ran the fifty-lap race driving 50 second laps, to Burman's 51.4 seconds. The next year, 1912, Kulick drove his Super T, renamed the 999 II, in honor of Henry Ford's earlier racer,

sprinting across Lake St. Clair at 103.4 mph, with a mechanic companion, and 107.8 mph solo, breaking Ford's own record set in 1904 in the original 999.

The next summer, Kulick, in a stripped but stock Model T, won the Algonquin Hill Climb for the second time. Competitors threatened the rules committee to disqualify Kulick from further events but this proved unnecessary for, by this time, Ford decided to abandon racing, feeling it was becoming too dangerous. This was not done, however, before Ford's attempt to enter the 999 II in the Indy 500 in 1913. When the officials demanded that the car meet a minimum weight regulation by adding 1,000 lb., Ford is reputed to have said, "We're building race cars, not trucks," as he ordered his entry back to the factory.

A 1922 "Foursum" body by the addition of a rumble seat. If this wasn't your "bag," one of their other roadster, speedster or touring designs probably was.

This 1926 ad was obviously one of the last to offer Model T replacement bodies—did the factory one better with their bodies available with "Two-tone snappy colors."

Chapter 9

The Modern 1926 Model T

Victor W. Pagé

Too little, too late – or, You can paint up a barn,
but it's still a barn and not a parlor

Body design changes

Body changes and chassis refinements more pronounced than any made since the adoption of the Model T chassis in 1908 have been announced for 1926 by the Ford Motor Company. With the announcement came the statement that there would be no changes in prices.

Outstanding features of the improvements in both open and closed types are lower and longer all-steel bodies on a chassis which has been reduced 1½-in. in height; complete new design in most body types; a change from black to green and maroon in the closed cars; larger, lower fenders; newly designed seats and larger and more powerful brakes. The composite wood work and steel panel construction is retained in the Fordor body.

The increased length of the improved models is still further accentuated by the new body lines in combination with a higher radiator and redesigned cowl. Wide crown fenders hung close to the wheels contribute to the general effect of lowness and smartness. While the runabout and touring car remain in black, the closed bodies are finished in colors and have nickel finished radiator shells. The Coupe and Tudor bodies are in deep channel green, while the Fordor is finished in Windsor maroon.

Greater driving comfort

Greater comfort is provided for driver and passengers in both open and closed cars by larger compartments, more deeply cushioned seats and greater leg room. In all models except the Fordor, a filler is hidden from sight by a cover similar to the cowl ventilator. One-piece windshields and narrowed pillars in the Tudor and Coupe give better visibility and ventilation.

Driving comfort has been increased by lower seats, improved back rests and lower steering wheel. Brake and clutch pedals are wider and more conveniently spaced. The open models now have a door at

A 1914 ad for aftermarket wheels for the Model T.

the left of the driver and side curtains, held secure by rods, open with the doors. Cord tires are standard equipment on all models, balloon cords being furnished as an option at extra cost. The reduction of 1½-in. in chassis height has been effected without materially decreasing the road clearance.

Coil box moved to engine

The coil box has been removed from the dash and now is mounted on the left-hand side of the engine, which change makes it unnecessary to enter the driving compartment to make adjustments. This arrangement is similar to that used for some time on the Fordson tractor power plant. The fan has been raised and the adjustment for fan belt tension improved. The fan bracket is now an integral part of the cylinder head outlet and is provided with an eccentric adjustment.

Improved and enlarged brakes

One of the most important improvements is in the brakes. The transmission brake band has been increased from 1⅛- to 1¾-in. width, this change resulting in smoother braking and longer life and less frequent adjustment of the bands. All transmission bands now have removable ears to facilitate replacement and hardened steel shoes have been placed over the clutch casing keys to prevent wear.

Brake drums at the rear axle have been increased to 11-in. diameter from 8-in. and width has been increased from 1- to 1½-in. The brake shoes now have coverings of an asbestos composition material, eliminating the old method in which braking was effected by direct contact with iron shoes.

In all models except the Fordor, the steering wheel has been dropped three inches for greater driving ease, as the seats have been moved back and lowered.

Gasoline tank under cowl

The new gasoline tank located under the cowl, which is used on all models except the Fordor, feeds gasoline to the carburetor at an abrupt angle and ensures fuel supply even on the steepest grades. A large trough and overflow pipe has been provided at the filler to carry any spillage directly to the ground. This change places the sediment bulb in the tank under the hood in a readily accessible position. Adequate separation of the fuel tank from the engine is provided by the dash.

The new crown fenders, in addition to being wider and larger, extend further down front and rear to afford better protection against splashing. The running boards on all models are wider and nearer to the ground.

Standard equipment in accessories on all closed cars includes windshield wiper, rear view mirror,

windshield visor and dash light. The dome light is continued in the Fordor and windshield wipers are supplied on the open models.

On the Tudor and Coupe, the windshield is a one-piece design opening forward. A passageway at the base of the shield directs ventilation downward into the front compartment when the windshield is slightly opened. The open models have a double ventilating type of windshield, both halves opening, and the Fordor shield has been redesigned to conform with the new cowl. The lower half of the windshield on this model is stationary and there is no cowl ventilator as before.

Hood is larger

The radiator is ⅝-in. higher and the hood is now larger with more louvers. The closed model windows are plate glass and lower flush with the moldings. Doors on all models open forward with the exception of the rear doors of the Fordor.

A new design of arm type tire carrier is provided which accommodates either the new Ford wire wheels or the demountable rim. The headlights have polished nickel rims, are set higher and further apart, and are attached to pressed steel fender supports.

Upholstery of new models

Tudor upholstery is gray fabric with fine green stripe to harmonize with the deep channel green exterior finish. Head linings are gray as is the silk back curtain and the carpet is greenish gray.

In the Coupe, which has the same upholstery as the Tudor, the rear deck has been made the full width of the body and extends well back over the rear spring with fenders bolted to the body, with resultant increase in the storage space available at this point. The shelf at the back of the seat is five inches deeper and the doors are also broader.

In the Fordor model, the upholstery fabric is gray with a fine red stripe to match with the new maroon exterior finish. Head linings and silk window curtains are gray and the carpet also is gray with a suggestion of red. The height of this model is 1½-in. less, due to the chassis changes, but otherwise there are no different dimensions.

The rear deck of the Roadster has been redesigned along the same lines as the Coupe. This model now has two doors, both of which are wider. The seat has been redesigned to give more comfort and a reduction of 2½-in. in height from the floor has been made.

Doors are wider

The touring model has a door at the driver's left and all four doors are wider. Seat contours have been improved. Three inches have been added to the width of the front seat and five to the rear. The distance between the back panel and the front of the rear seat has been increased 3½-in.

In bringing out the improved models, the Ford Motor Co. is cautioning its dealers against the word "new." It is pointed out that, while it is true that these are more radical and more conspicuous than any that heretofore have been made, the Model T chassis, though lower, remains basically the same as it has been since 1908. The objection to the use of the word "new" is based on the fact that it implies a redesigning of the chassis as well as the body. As far as can be ascertained, there have been no changes in the power plant, notwithstanding the many rumors that have been circulating in automotive circles and no changes have been spoken of by the makers. As a matter of fact, changes are not spoken of lightly when a factory is equipped with special production machinery that makes 10,000 cars a day output possible.

It is apparent that the effort of the Ford engineers has been to concentrate chiefly on obtaining greater beauty and comfort in design. An analysis of the cars shows that most of the changes have been influenced by this factor. The only important mechanical change has been made in the brakes. Greater convenience and comfort for driver and passengers has resulted from moving the fuel tank to its new position under the cowl, increasing the size of the seats and providing more leg room, lowering the steering wheel, adding an extra door to the Touring car and Runabout, and placing the brake and clutch pedals farther apart and providing each with a flange to keep the foot from slipping.

New type transmission bands

It is no longer necessary to remove the transmission cover to change the new type of bands. A detachable ear on each side allows the bands to be withdrawn and replaced through the transmission cover door. The ear is held in place by studs in the ear slots, the shoulder of the car snapping over the end of the brake band, thus holding it securely in place. To remove the ear, it is only necessary to insert a tool, which is made by bending over the end of a screw driver one-quarter of an inch, through the end of the ear into the square hole in the end of the brake band, lifting up on the tool and forcing the band down and the ear back. After the nuts, washers and springs have been removed from the pedal shafts, the reverse and brake pedals are pulled out as far as possible, removing the ears, as explained. The bands then may be withdrawn, from the right side, permitting them to follow close to the cover, to prevent their distortion. When a car is equipped with the old type of bands, the transmission cover must be removed. The slow speed shaft must be cut off about ⅞

of an inch from the shoulder and the new type slow speed adjusting screw installed.

New steering gear reduction

Steering gears of 5:1 ratio, originally installed only in cars equipped with balloon tires, now are being used on all cars regardless of tire equipment. A new steering wheel, 17 inches in diameter, is used with the improved steering gears, which, together with the increased ratio, add materially to steering control. The gears used in the new 5:1 steering arrangement are not interchangeable with the old 4:1 type, and it is important that mechanics understand the difference in ratios, to prevent accidents due to locking.

Ford generator and battery troubles

The Ford generator is of the simplest possible construction. Indications of trouble in the generator are first ascertained by reading the ammeter. At normal driving speeds (about 20 miles per hour) the pointer or needle should register between 8 and 12 amperes charge on the scale. If there is less charge than this or no charge, the difficulty may result from a fault in the generator, the cutout, or the external wiring circuit.

Trouble in the external wiring is due to one of the following causes, which may be found by careful inspection:

(a) Poor or loose connection at the terminals in the wiring circuit between the generator and the battery.

(b) Broken wire, either at the terminal or inside the insulation.

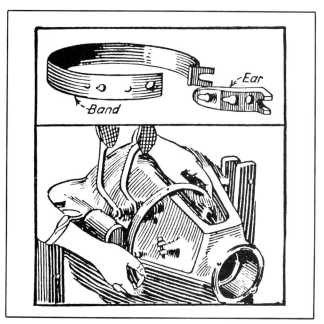

Above, the new style transmission band with a detachable ear. Below, a method of removing the band without the need to take off the upper part of transmission cover.

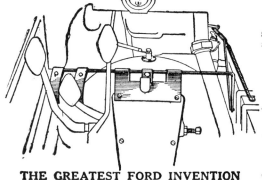
A 1921 ad for a Speederator, apparently a device to transfer lever-controlled gas and spark feed to foot-control. It appears to have been a big failure, as this is the only ad for the device ever found.

(c) Grounded wire due to defective insulation. To determine whether or not the trouble lies in the generator, attach the positive (+) wire of a direct current (D.C.) meter registering from 0 to 30 volts, to the terminal on the generator, and the negative (-) wire to the yoke (housing) of the generator. With the engine running at normal speed (20 miles per hour) the instrument should read 7 volts or more.

If a volt meter is not available, another method used for determining whether or not the trouble lies in

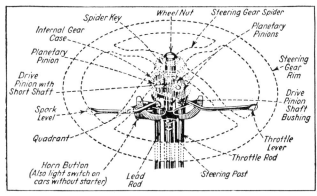

The new-type steering gear showing planetary reduction gears and their relation to wheel.

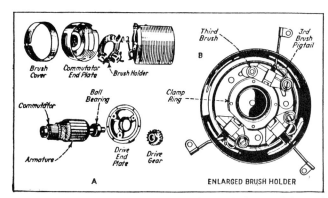

How a Ford generator looks when dismantled at A. Enlarged commutator plate end with brush holder in place at B.

the generator is by grounding the generator terminal by connecting it with the generator yoke, using a screw driver or some other piece of metal to short circuit the current. If no spark occurs at the moment of grounding, the generator is not producing current.

If the volt meter shows less than 7 volts, disconnect the wire attached to the cutout and unscrew the three cap screws which hold the generator to the gear case. The generator is now free of the engine and may be removed by prying it off with a screw driver, forcing the generator out and down until the gears disengage.

The trouble may be due to one of the following causes:

(1) dirty commutator (points); (2) brush spring weak or binding; (3) brushes not seating properly; (4) brushes not touching commutator; (a) held up by spring, (b) sticking in holder, (c) worn too short; (5) Short-circuited in the armature or field; (6) ground in brush wires, field or armature; (7) open circuit in field, armature or brushes.

Besides the electrical trouble, the generator is subject to mechanical wear as follows: (1) commutator, (a) segments rough, (b) under-size brushes—brushes rubbing on mica; (2) ball bearings broken or worn; (3) brush ring loose and shifting; (4) third brush carrier shifting.

Setting third brush

First, shift the third brush to the left as far as possible, that is, toward the engine, then loosen the four screws which lock the brush holder assembly in position approximately half a turn, which will allow the brush holder assembly to be moved freely in each direction. Care should be taken not to run out these threads more than necessary to allow the brush holder assembly to move freely. If the screws are run out too far the clamp ring will fall off inside the generator and replacing it would necessitate removing the generator. Next, start the engine, opening the throttle until the engine is running at a speed equivalent to approximately 20 miles per hour, then rotate the brush holder assembly until the ammeter indicates the maximum output. Next, tighten the screws which hold the brush holder assembly in position, then shift the third brush until the ammeter shows 12 amperes charge, then tighten the third brush nut.

Once the adjustment has been set and the four screws tightened, the adjustment should never be changed unless a new armature or brush holder assembly is installed. It is, of course, understood that the third brush can be shifted to meet varying conditions. For instance, a car that is driven only on short trips necessitates frequent starting with consequent drain on the battery, would require a higher charging rate than

the car that is driven only on long runs. For average conditions, however, a charging rate of 12 amperes is the most suitable.

If, for any reason, the engine is run with the generator disconnected from the battery, as on a block test, or when the battery has been removed for repair or recharging, be sure that the generator is grounded by running a wire from the terminal on generator to one of the dust cover screws in the yoke. Two strands of shipping wire may be used for this purpose. Be sure that the connections at both ends of the wire are tight. Failure to do this when the engine is running with the generator disconnected from the battery will result in serious injury to the generator. *Never ground the generator through the cutout!*

Lubricating the new Ford

In Fig. 5 is outlined the principal points of the Ford chassis needing lubrication and represents the advice of factory service experts. Careful study of this chart will prove valuable. All oil cups should be sup-

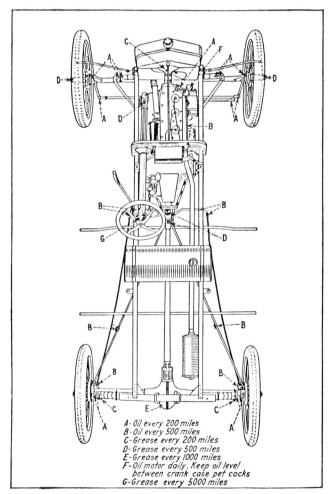

A - Oil every 200 miles
B - Oil every 500 miles
C - Grease every 200 miles
D - Grease every 500 miles
E - Grease every 1000 miles
F - Oil motor daily. Keep oil level
      between crank case pet cocks
G - Grease every 5000 miles

Lubrication chart outlining vital lubricating points and lubricating schedules.

plied with the same light grade lubricating oil used in the engine and all "dope" cups should be filled periodically as indicated, with good, free-flowing cup grease. The commutator should be kept freely supplied with oil at all times and should be cleaned out of "gummy" about every 500 miles, wiped clean and reoiled with fresh lubricant.

When it is advisable to fill dope cup covers, screw them down, refill the grease and repeat the operation two or three times. Always open the oil cups by turning them to the right as this keeps tightening rather than loosening them. A drop of oil now and then in the crank handle bearing is also necessary. The Ford Motor Company recommends only medium grade gas engine oil for use in all Model T engines when new. In cold weather, a light grade of oil having a low cold test is absolutely necessary for adequate lubrication of the engine. Graphite should not be used in either engine or transmission as it will have a short-circuiting effect on the magneto.

It is also advised by factory experts, to clean out the crankcase by draining off the dirty oil when the new car has been driven 350 miles, thereafter it will only be necessary to repeat the operation every 750 miles. Remove the plug under the flywheel casing and the oil will run out. Replace the plug and pour about one gallon of kerosene in through the breather pipe. Turn the engine over with the starting motor for fifteen or twenty seconds, or with the hand crank for thirty or forty revolutions, so the splash from the kerosene will cleanse all internal engine parts.

Again, remove the crankcase plug and drain off the oil/kerosene mixture. Make sure that all the kerosene is removed from the depressions in the crankcase by putting a quart of lubricating oil into the motor after the drain plug is replaced then turn the engine crankshaft several times as mentioned to mix the kerosene and flushing oil, then remove the crankcase plug for the last time to drain out the flushing mixture. Refill with fresh oil until it runs slowly from the upper pet cock.

Do not make the mistake of putting too much grease in the differential housing. This should not be more than one-third full. If fluid grease is used, the level should be approximately one and a half inches below the oil hole. This plug should be removed about every 1,000 miles and more grease added if necessary. While the chart presented specifies that the fan be lubricated with grease every 200 miles, this applies only to cars having fans equipped with grease cups. The new style magazine oiler fans should be lubricated by unscrewing the oil plug and filling the hub, which is hollow, to form a reservoir or magazine, with a heavy but fluid oil.

Primers to make starting easy

Difficulty is sometimes experienced in starting automobiles in cold weather because the fuel does not vaporize quickly enough and will not explode. A simple accessory that combines three distinct devices in one, as it is a primer, an electric vaporizer and sprayer, and an economizer is being marketed. This can be seen in the accompanying drawing for the Model T. A simple priming cup on the dashboard is connected to the electric vaporizer on the inlet manifold by a short piece of copper tubing. The resistance coil in the plug may be heated by either storage battery or dry cells. Gasoline is put into the priming cup and passes through the heated plug, with the result that as the engine is cranked over a hot vapor that is easily ignited is supplied the cylinders and the engine will start as easily in cold weather as in warm. The priming cock may be opened to act as an auxiliary air valve and gasoline saver after the engine has warmed up, if desired.

Vapor humidifiers

A number of accessory makers are exploiting devices to admit steam or water in with the mixture

A 1920 ad for the do-it-yourself mechanic-driver.

which is said to reduce carbon deposits, and so on. In A in the accompanying drawing, warm, moist air is supplied to the manifold, the exact amount being controlled from the dash. It consists of a valve at the manifold from which runs a pipe to the filler spout of the radiator, from which point the vapor is procured. It is said to provide a better mixture and, consequently, to improve the power and smoothness of operation of the engine. The Gemco steam vaporizer, shown at B in the illustration, is fastened to the top of the exhaust manifold and delivers steam to the intake manifold. The wa-

ter is held within a sealed container and begins to give off vapor as soon as the exhaust pipe is heated. The regular water system is the source of supply and the vaporizer needs no attention once it is installed.

The Marsh device, shown at C, consists of connecting the overflow pipe of the radiator through a combination and three-way spring check or compensating valve to the intake manifold above the carburetor. It is operated by a rod leading to the dash. By turning the plug of the valve, air can be drawn from the radiator interior, or from the outside, or from both sources at the same time, or cut out entirely as condi-

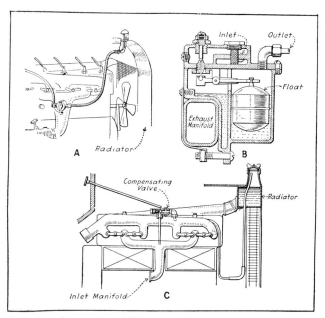

Electrically heated vaporizer for easier starting.

A group of vapor humidifiers to reduce carbon deposits.

A 1924 ad for a vapor humidifier claiming outstanding mileage achieved with its use.

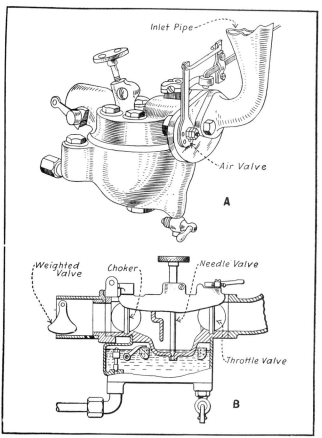

Fuel economizer device used in connection with Model T carburetor.

tions require. The radiator connection is to obtain water vapor to stimulate combustion in the motor. When alcohol is used for winter driving it is claimed that the vapor from this liquid will still further assist combus-

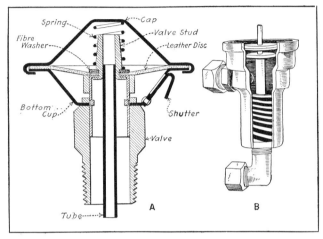

Auxiliary air valves for attachment to the inlet manifold.

tion. The spring check is to prevent water from entering the motor when it is not running.

Fuel economizing devices

The increasing cost of fuel has resulted in the development of many devices, some automatic, others manually controlled to admit extra air into the intake manifold and thin out the gas mixture at medium and high engine speeds, thereby securing greater economy. Great claims are made for the efficiency of these devices but they do not always live up to the expectations of their makers. Some work out very well in practice and savings in fuel consumption have been secured ranging from 5 to 20 per cent, by their use. The compensating vapor plug, a cross-section of which is shown at A of the accompanying illustration, is intended to screw into the manifold, and its purpose is to feed fresh air to the gas charge coming from the carburetor in such proportions as to conduct a charge to the motor which will be most efficient as regards gasoline consumption and power developed. This action is automatic, air being sucked in by the action of the piston in quantities depending on the speed of the motor.

A 1927 Touring Model T—the last of the line.

The Duplex air valve, shown at B, is a similar device, intended to be screwed into the intake manifold. The casting houses the valve opening into the manifold, the valve being operated by a piston working in a cylinder, which is also connected to the manifold. At low speeds, the valve is held closed by vacuum, but at higher speeds the reduced vacuum allows the valve to open under the action of a spring, admitting additional air.

An automatic gasoline economizer for Ford cars which is installed between the inlet pipe and carburetor without drilling, tapping or machine work, is seen in the accompanying drawing at A. It consists of a hollow chamber with a passage communicating between the inlet pipe and a peculiar valve which is connected by a simple linkage to the throttle rod, and operates with every movement of the throttle, its purpose being to admit pure air which dilutes the overrich mixture and effectively vaporizes the heavy ends. It is not dependent upon foot or hand control, and as it is claimed the proportion of air admitted is absolutely correct for each opening of the throttle, installation may be accomplished in 10 minutes.

The Myle-Maker, seen in the illustration at B, is an attachment to go onto the standard Ford carburetor and for which the claim is made that the gas mileage will be increased from 3 to 10 miles per gallon. The device is a gravity-operated flutter valve controlling the richness of the gas mixture in inverse ratio to the speed of the engine. There is only one moving part; a composition metal hinge or gate valve, suspended at the top and filling a square space through which air passes. At low engine speeds, the hinge remains suspended vertically, allowing enough air to pass underneath it to afford a suitably rich mixture. This is said to facilitate cranking and idling. As the motor is speeded up, the suction of the engine pulls the valve in, allowing more air to enter the carburetor and consequently diluting the mixture. When much gas is needed to start a cold engine, the flutter valve remains partially closed, automatically richening the mixture. When the engine is running freely, the valve is lifted by engine suction and the mixture is automatically thinned out.

Editor's note

As already pointed out by the author, a very considerable number of changes went into the 1926 Model T, making it virtually a new car, "except for the chassis" which the factory was careful to point out was the same as the original 1908 design. This was hardly anything to boast about, in 1926.

Despite all these changes, however, including the nickel-plated radiator shell, new color options and balloon tires as standard equipment, the public's response was much less than hoped for by the factory. Business fell off to such an extent that it is reported that seven out of ten Ford dealers lost money in 1926. The common consensus seems to have been something like "You can paint up a barn, but it's still a barn and not a parlor."

As usual in the automobile industry, serious thought about an entirely new model to replace the failing Model T was inaugurated at the last minute. Quite obviously, only the vaguest of replacement plans for the Model T were ever entertained by Ford. He almost naively expected the T to go on forever and even when committed to an entirely new design is said to have remarked that the Model T was still the car that the public should have.

On May 25, 1927, the official announcement was made by the Ford Motor Company that an entirely new model was being developed.

Chapter 10

Running the Ford on Fuel Oil

A very efficient and simple fuel oil conversion
for Model T Ford motors, for use on power
outfits, tractor jobs, etc., where hours of
continuous operation are required, can be
built at a cost not exceeding $1.50

A Ford Model T converted into a tractor to burn fuel oil (kerosene).

The only parts needed for this fuel oil conversion of a Ford engine, other than standard equipment, are four feet of 1½″ flexible heater hose and about five feet of ¼″ copper tubing.

First, remove the exhaust and intake manifolds, and replace them in an inverted position; the carburetor and hot air intake can then be bolted in place. A 2″ piece of regular exhaust pipe, with flange, is cut off and held in place with a large hexagon nut. This is used to couple the flexible tube to the exhaust manifold; the tube, however, should not be put in place until the manifold cover is put in place. This shield which keeps the intake manifold hot and supplies hot air for the carburetor is taken from a piece of sheet metal 12″ by 18″ and cut as shown. Twist the end of the flexible tube in the reverse direction to that in which it is wound and it will enlarge enough to slip over the short piece of exhaust pipe.

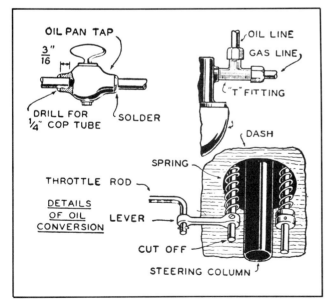

The simple changes illustrated on these two drawings are the only requirements to convert a Model T for fuel oil use.

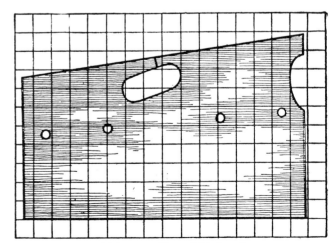

Pattern for manifold cover. The grid is in 1 in. squares.

A close-up view of the completed conversion. Note the copper tubing wound around the new exhaust manifold (seen in center of exhaust manifold, with copper tubing leading off to left).

Rear side of the conversion, showing connections to the carburetor.

Two fuel tanks are needed: one for gas, when starting, and the other for fuel oil. A two-chamber tank is used in the original, but a gallon varnish can would serve for the gas tank. The gas line goes directly from the tank to the tee fitting (in place of the usual elbow) in the carburetor; while the fuel-oil line goes from the large tank to the exhaust tube, where it is given eight or nine turns, and then to the tee in the carburetor.

The carburetor throttle rod should be bent, as shown in the drawing, from a piece of $\frac{3}{16}''$ rod and drilled in each end for a small cotter pin. Next, cut off the carburetor control rod, one inch below the small spring in front of the dash; then remove the little pin and cupped washer, and replace with the small lever arm, leaving the spring in place.

A Ford oil-pan tap is used on each fuel line, to make it possible to switch from one fuel to the other.

The choke is connected by a wire to the dash control, with a small opposing coil spring fastened to a manifold stud.

If this conversion is to be used in a tractor, the dash should be braced, as shown in the photographs, to support the extra strain caused by the weight of the fuel tank on top. In any case, the tanks must be kept high enough for the fuel to flow by gravity.

To operate, see that the tap in fuel oil line is turned off; let the carburetor fill up with gas, and start; let the motor warm up thoroughly for ten minutes; then turn the fuel oil on, and gas off. Watch the motor carefully while changing fuels, and adjust the mixture to suit, until engine is running smoothly. It is well to release any load from the motor when changing from fuel oil to gas.

In stopping, turn off the fuel and let the motor run until it has consumed all the fuel oil in the carburetor; or shut off the fuel and ignition and drain the carburetor. All the fuel oil must be drained out of the carburetor before attempting to restart the engine, as it cannot be started on fuel oil very satisfactorily.

It is advisable not to use a water pump when using fuel oil, as much better combustion will be obtained when the engine is running hot.

(*Mechanics and Handicraft*, July 1936. Oscar H. Gibson.)

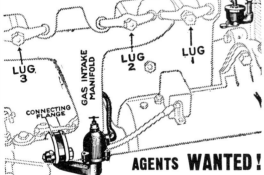

Chapter 11

Connecting Electric Accessories on the Automobile

John Jackson tells you how: "It's an easy job."

"Where's J.J.?" asked Bill Smith, alighting from his car at the door of John Jackson's garage.

"In the shop" replied Hank, J.J.'s gas and oil attendant and general handy man, as he unlocked the gasoline pump. "Anything I can do for you? You must be in a hurry this morning, you're around so early."

"No," replied Bill. "I just want J.J. to wire up my spotlight. You know I've got to go over to Centerville tonight, and J.J. didn't have a spotlight in the house last night, so I bought one over at the hardware store, and they didn't know how to wire it."

"You've been driving a car for five years, Bill. Why don't you wire it up yourself?" broke in a voice behind them, as J.J. strolled out of the garage. "It's an easy job."

"Maybe it is, John, but I don't know how to do it" replied Bill.

"Well, gimmie the works, and I'll show you how it's done" remarked J.J., "and then, when you buy a cigar lighter, or some other gadget in another town, where they haven't a good-natured garageman to wire it up for you, you can do the job yourself.

"Connecting a spotlight, hand warmer or any other kind of electrical device on a car is extremely simple," said J.J. as he started to work. "Most accessories of this kind have switches of their own, the spotlight usually having a switch in the handle. Practically all cars nowadays have the single-wire or grounded wiring system, and this also makes the wiring of accessories a simple matter. The first thing to do, of course, is to decide on the position of the accessory, and mount it. Convenience is usually the thing to be consulted in this.

"Some drivers prefer their spotlight on their own side where they can adjust it while driving, and others

Connecting accessories to the Ford T manifold terminal block.

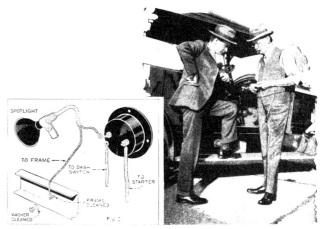

Ends of all wires should be bared and scraped clean and all frame contacts polished.

133

mount it on the right side of the windshield and adjust it to the side of the road, then let it go. On the right side, it annoys approaching drivers somewhat less than when on the left, but, on the other hand, it cannot then be used to read sign posts or house numbers. For my part, I prefer it mounted down below the headlights, on the front of the car, directed on the right-hand edge of the road. In this position, it gives the maximum light where it is most wanted, and can't glare into an approaching motorist's eyes. For reading signs, I have another spot mounted on the windshield frame.

"Having mounted the device where you want it, one of the wires is connected to the frame. The proper way to do this is to remove the nut and washer from a convenient bolt on the frame—and the bolt, too, if possible—clean off the rust and paint from the frame member around the bolt and brighten it with a file or emery cloth, polish the under side of the washer with the emery cloth also, skin the wire and brighten it, loop it around the bolt—so—then place the washer back with the bright side against the wire. This makes a good clean connection. A light coat of shellac over the joint is an additional precaution against corrosion, but care should be taken not to put on such a coat that the shellac will creep between the wire and the frame or washer and ruin the connection.

"Now the other wire can be connected, so run it to one side of the ammeter. There are two terminals on the ammeter, and if the wire is connected to one terminal, the current consumed by the accessory will regis-

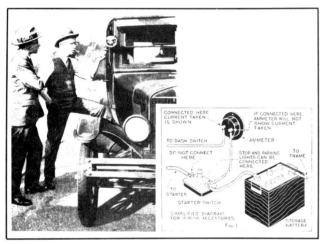

Here is a simplified diagram of wiring involved in connecting accessories on the car.

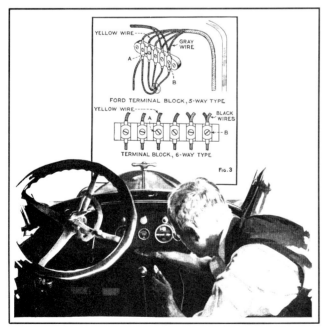

Testing on the ammeter terminals before tightening. Above, connections for the newer Ford system with six terminals.

ter on the instrument; if connected to the other, it won't. If it is a heater that is being attached, like a carburetor heater, it is better that the current doesn't pass through the ammeter, as it is usually somewhat heavy, and might injure it. Switch on your spotlight. Now we'll try the end of the wire on this terminal. It doesn't show any reading?

"All right, we'll try it on the other. It shows now, doesn't it? There, she's tight. That's all there's to it. If it doesn't register when connected to one terminal, try the other. What if you don't know which is the 'on' position of the accessory switch? Oh, that's easy. Just wire temporarily directly to the battery terminals and try the switch both ways; that'll soon show which way is the right position.

"I remember that the first car I had to put a spotlight on had no ammeter. I was kind o' green at this electrical game at the time, and it struck me. My boss showed me how to do it, though, and it was just as simple as this job. He first found the 'on' position of the switch, in the way I just mentioned, and turned it on. Then he turned the lighting and ignition switch on the instrument board off, and connected one wire from the spotlight to the frame, just like this. Then he started touching the bared end of the other wire to the terminals on the back of the lighting switch until he found where the spot would light up, and that was the one he connected it to. If you ever run into a car like that, however, be sure that the accessory switch is turned on, or you'll be likely to hunt a long time for the right terminal.

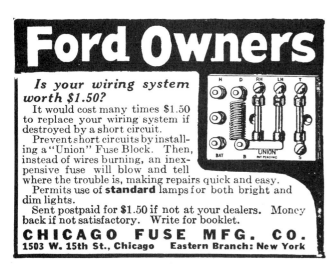
"Is your wiring system worth $150?"

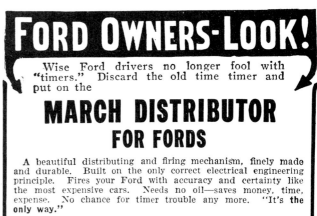
Ad for March Distributors for "wise Ford drivers."

Bullet-head Apco lights "improve the looks of the car 100%."

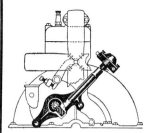
Elevated timer bracket relocated timer to left-hand side of engine.

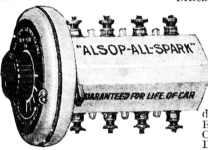
The Alsop-All-Spark was an electrical cure-all for $7.50.

Just Rite roller timer and Just Rite Foot Accelerator ad.

"A stoplight or parking light may sometimes be more conveniently connected to one side of the starting switch, but be sure to connect it on the battery side of the switch, where the battery is connected to the ammeter. In this case, of course, the current taken by the light is not registered on the ammeter.

"There is another way to connect a spotlight that has some advantages. The spot is usually trained on the right-hand side of the road, and in many cases it is not used when the bright lights are on, the driver turning on the spotlight when he switches from bright to dim on meeting another car. This means two motions. If the spotlight wire is connected to the terminal on the back of the lighting switch that supplies current for the dim lights or for the small side lights, the act of switching from bright to dim will turn on the spot at the same time. On the Ford, this connection may be made at the connection block or manifold at the front of the dash. On the older type, the connection block has five terminals, and the spotlight is connected to the second one from the left—the one carrying the yellow wire—if the light is to be connected to the battery at all times.

Jefferson Magneto Lamp Regulator and lighting system.

"If you want it on with the dim lights only, connect it to the terminal on the extreme right. This terminal carries a yellow wire – if you can make out the color. On the newer Fords, the block has six terminals, and the third from the left, carrying the yellow wires, gives a direct battery connection. The one on the right, as before (but now carrying black wires) connects the light to the dim circuit.

"Suppose you forget which terminal is which? That's easy. In that case, the lighting switch is turned to the 'dim' position and the end of the wire touched to the terminals on the block, in turn, until the one is found that will light up the spot. To make sure that it is the right one, switch to 'bright' and see if the spotlight goes out. If it does, it's OK; if not, you'll have to try again, as you may have hit the horn terminal, or some other one.

"Connecting stoplights? Well, there are a number of ways to do the job, but the simplest way for the average owner is to connect one wire, from the stoplight switch, to one side of the starting switch and the other wire to one of the terminals on the stoplight socket. The other socket terminal is grounded to the frame. If you want to have an indicator that will show whether or not the stoplight is working, and I advise this, for a stoplight that isn't working is worse than none at all, then you can install another dash-light socket carrying a 2-cp. bulb, on the instrument board. Run one wire from the ammeter terminal to one on the dash socket, and another wire from the socket to the stoplight switch, then to the light, which is grounded to the

frame. You can color the dash bulb red so that it will show up strongly whenever the light is operated.

"When you get a stoplight, examine the switch and see that it is well made, for the switch is usually the weakest part of the installation, and most of the stoplights that aren't working have inoperative switches.

"Most accessories are connected by means of flexible cords and these will kink and fray, leading eventually to breaks and short circuits. See that the wires are stapled to the body or fastened to the frame firmly. Wires leading inside the car can be sewed to the upholstery, and this is usually the neatest way to fasten them.

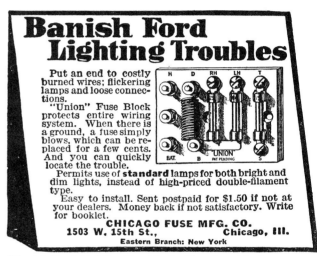
"Banish Ford Lighting Troubles" with a fuse block.

"Classy" Ford lighting outfits.

Under the car, they can be stapled to the floorboards. If armored wire is used, slip a short length of rubber tubing over it wherever it touches the frame of the sheet metal body, so as to prevent rattles that may prove difficult to find some time in the future.

"There you are, Bill, all set. No trouble at all, only next time, let me sell you the accessory, as well as install it for you. Sure, I hadn't any spotlight yesterday, but I'll have them this afternoon. So long!" (*Popular Mechanics*, June 1926.)

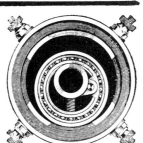

138

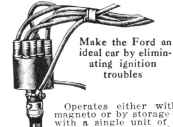

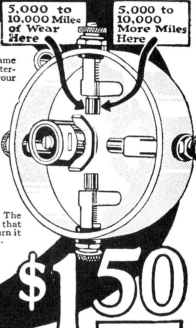

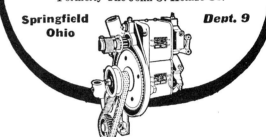
141

Chapter 12

Model T Antitheft Devices

"Almost in the time it takes you to step into a
cigar store for a box of your favorite Havanas,
the crook can wire your switch and be gone"

"If a convenient method of locking the car is desired, get a piece of good heavy chain about a foot long and a suitable padlock. To lock the car, open the throttle and advance the spark levers as far as they will go, passing the chain about both levers and inside one of the notched segments, and with the lock connect the ends of the chain and it is safe to say no joy rider will get consolation out of your car."

Thus concludes the suggestions of *The American Motorist* in their March 1925 issue entitled "Making Car Stealing Unprofitable."

It began by stating that "Car theft in 1924 was nearly 50 percent greater in twenty-eight key cities than in 1923 and more than one hundred percent greater than in 1918. In 1924 the report is encourag-

ing, however, in that it demonstrates that while the number of thefts is increasing, which is to be expected with several million new cars put on the road annually the percentage of recovery shows improvement each year."

The main thrust of the article was to advocate a "vigorous campaign to secure a universal State certificate-of-title law," which the magazine believed

A 1924 ad for an antitheft device which produces whistlelike sounds and "automatically kills your engine dead."

A 1921 ad offering a unique means of preventing your Model T from being stolen—at least it requires no secret switches.

"will ultimately destroy the market for stolen cars and reduce the cost of automobile insurance."

It is interesting to observe that the cost of automobile insurance was of concern to 1925 motorists. The article concluded by saying, "If there is no market, there is no money in stealing automobiles."

The *American Motorist* ran a similar article in its October 1925 article entitled, "My Car—It's Gone!" The story began with the car thief's basic philosophy: "Keys are convenient things to have, but like so many other things in life, they're not absolutely necessary." The article itself admitted that "even the best lock cannot hope to be more than something that occasions delay . . . [A]n ignition lock will delay a thief and delay may mean detection. Yet, almost in the time it takes you to step into a cigar store . . . for a box of your favorite Havanas, the crook can wire your switch and be gone. A car that cannot be steered with the wheel, or one whose transmission is locked in neutral may be towed to a place where ample time may be taken to fix matters."

An interesting example of car theft—if there is such a thing—followed. "Not long ago a man who had a wire-wheeled car thought he'd put one over on the thieves when he passed a chain through his front wheel and locked this chain around a telegraph pole. When he returned from his errand, all he found was the wheel which was still chained to the pole. The thief had taken the front wheel from the axle and replaced it with the spare which the owner carried in the rear. Perfectly simple!"

Another similar case: "One motorist with a high-priced car, figured he should follow a scheme lauded by Chicago's chief of police . . . who advises everyone to remove the rotor from the ignition distributor. Our man had done that very thing, yet his car had been taken. How? The thief, lifting the hood to see why the engine wouldn't start, saw the distributor latches were down and that the rotor was out. Just then an owner of a similar car, who had parked a few cars behind the victim, but had taken the precaution to lock his steering gear, found himself unable to start. Investigation proved that his ignition rotor had been removed and, no doubt, was used by the thief in getting away with the first car."

A third case started with, "Even the drop-forged horseshoelike affair which had quite a vogue a short time ago, was clamped around the wheel, was circumvented by thieves who, once they selected their prey, secured a wheel ostensibly meant to get a crippled car to the garage and, replacing the horseshoe-clad wheel with the repair wheel, they made away with the car of their selection." This same type of device is used today to prevent ticketed cars from being driven off from no parking areas. In one instance, reported in the papers,

the ticketed car had disappeared. All that was left was the horsehoe-like device, which had been hack-sawed in two!

As the article concluded, "As delay seems to be all that can be hoped for in equipping a car with theft protection, those of the motoring clan who may be inclined to resort to homemade devices find the electrical system a willing ally." Several methods of forestalling car theft via homemade electrical devices were then explained.

The following four are from *Popular Mechanics* magazine. A 1927 issue ran an article entitled "Concealed Switch Prevents Theft." The copy stated, "The concealed switch device . . . is a means of disconnecting the auto switch from the battery. It consists of a sleeve, made of hard insulating material, which contains a terminal with one threaded end, and another terminal with a knurled and threaded end, to which the wire is connected. The inside of the insulating sleeve is threaded to correspond to these parts. In use, the parts are turned in one direction to break the circuit and in the other to complete it. This switch can be used in most circuits."

In a 1932 issue, *Popular Mechanics* ran an article under the heading "Foiling Auto Thieves." Readers were told: "The auto ignition lock shown . . . embodies a simple method of making an auto thief pass up your car in preference to one that will start more easily. After he has shorted out the ignition switch, he does not anticipate another break in the wiring. Any ordinary cleat socket is screwed in some inconspicuous

A 1920 ad offering a "Fox-proof rigid steering wheel lock for Fords" as well as a means of preventing spare tire theft.

place, and is connected to the storage-battery circuit. Of course, the wires leading to the socket must be well concealed."

A 1936 issue contained an article entitled, "Dual Starter Switches Foil Thief Trying to Start Car." The article stated the author's experiences as follows: "I have an alarm on my car by which anyone pressing the starter switch sounds a loud horn. The secret lies in wiring the starter motor to an auxiliary switch placed well up on the floor boards where it is unnoticeable. A loud horn is wired to the regular switch, which would naturally be used by anyone unfamiliar with the arrangement."

A 1925 issue, anticipating some of the drawbacks to these do-it-yourself efforts to reduce or prevent car theft, revealed in an article entitled, "Secret Switch Prevents Car Theft," its solutions to obvious drawbacks.

The magazine explained, "With this snap-on jumper wire, a thief can readily bridge the ignition wires of a car, when the switch is thrown off, and complete

the circuit, which enables him to get away with the car. To prevent this, the autoist may have a secret switch, in addition to the regular one, but the thief after first bridging the regular switch, notices that there is no discharge on the ammeter, and so he finds the second switch and bridges this one, too.

"However, the switch and connection shown in the drawing will foil the expert car thief, as with this arrangement, the correct discharge is shown on the ammeter, after the regular switch has been bridged, but the coil is grounded so that the car cannot be operated. This is accomplished by mounting an extra switch behind the dash, of which one side is connected to the frame of the car and the other to the spark coil by carefully concealed wires. Ordinarily, when the car is running, this switch is open, but is closed to make the ignition system theft-proof."

The last of these suggestions on preventing car theft appeared in a 1953 issue under the heading, "Burglar Alarm for the Auto Tells Police it is Stolen." The copy began: "Stolen cars broadcast their own messages

A 1918 ad offering theft protection by means of a combination lock arrangement. Attached to the coil box, it prevented starting without knowledge of the combination—unless the thief short-circuited the device.

with the automatic burglar alarm which the thieves set off unwittingly. The alarm has the appearance of a licence plate and is attached to the front and rear of the car.

"It is connected to the starter and will flip the plate over if an attempt is made to start the car while the device is operating. When the plate is turned over, it displays a 'Help, Police' sign. Another button near the steering wheel will do the same thing if the driver presses it in the midst of a holdup."

An ad for a "New Electric Robot Cell" that would put "auto thieves on the spot" was advertised in 1931. Additional copy stated in smaller type, "No thief can touch your car or anything in it without starting a clamorous riot of noise that will not stop until he runs away." An illustration gave an exaggerated reaction of a would-be thief, obviously frightened by an actual voice coming from a car he was about to steal.

Johnson Smith & Company, noted for their mail-order novelties of the thirties, included in one of their

ads an "Auto Scare Bomb." In addition to emitting "a shrill whistle," when a transgressor stepped on a car's starter, "a loud bang" was said to result, giving the would-be thief the impression that the "car had exploded." At only fifteen cents, three for forty cents, the device was obviously a "steal."

An upgraded device of this sort appeared in 1982. It claimed superiority over other similar devices that "make noise" as a means of deterring car thieves. Since cars protected merely with a noise-making device were not immune to thieves making off with the car itself, the makers of Gard-A-Car offered a device that prevented thieves from moving the car. A timed circuit-breaker in the unit tripped within ten seconds after such a protected car was started by an unautho-

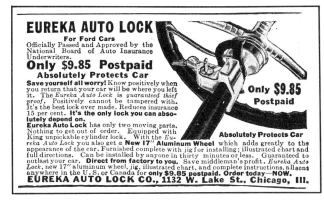

Another steering wheel lock attachment, equipped with a King "unpickable cylinder lock," so good it was guaranteed by the National Board of Auto Insurance Underwriters.

BRUTE FORCE and SCIENCE

1920

SPECIAL YALE CYLINDER

COMBINED

Only $7.⁰⁰

GOES ON LEFT WHEEL

"STOP THIEF"

Locks Ford and ALL Other Locks

We Say So With $100.00 Reward

ATTENTION
JOBBERS—DEALERS—OWNERS

STOP THIEF AUTO LOCK CO., BIRMINGHAM, ALA.

A 1920 device for immobilizing a Model T by securing the left front wheel, preventing turning.

Cartoon entitled "Absolutely burglar-proof," spoofing the hard-starting characteristics of the Model T.

rized person. This stalled the engine, which could not be started again until a switch was turned off and the reset button pushed "and only you know where the box (with the secret reset button) is hidden" said the ad. The noise-maker seems to have been the only kind of protection against car theft that has survived at least as far as all these devices and schemes are concerned. Even these are far from foolproof. Every once in a while, one can be heard going off at a local parking lot, with no one in sight.

A few more words are in order regarding the early antitheft devices before concluding this subject. One 1922 ad featured the assuring statement, "At last! A Real Steering Wheel Lock for Ford Cars!" In smaller type the ad continued: "It is not a loose wheel that 'spins.' Not a device to jam the steering mechanism— or weaken vital parts.

"Not a flimsy die cast structure to replace some important part on which your life depends—but a real 100% efficient securing device that locks instantly WITHOUT key, with gloves on or off, always in plain view, whether locked or unlocked.

"You do not have to buy a new wheel or change a single part to install, which is accomplished IN LESS THAN FIVE MINUTES WITH A SCREW DRIVER.

"Genuine YALE non-pickable lock and all parts made of strongest steel insures protection. Locks wheel in either straight ahead, right or left hand position as desired. It is forget proof, thief proof and accident proof. Pronounced by Automotive Authorities the greatest achievement ever accomplished in locking devices—such is the New York steering wheel lock for Ford cars."

"When swung upward by hand, wrist or elbow, powerful steel arms go between and over two spokes, not only preventing turning of wheel, but making removal of wheel impossible." Price was only $7.50, with "money refunded at the end of thirty days' trial, if you are not convinced that it is the best and most necessary investment you have ever made."

The other ad worth mentioning started with "If your engine can't breathe, your car won't go." That's the principle of The Venn Auto-Lock for Ford cars. Locks the passage of gas in the manifold. The surest and safest way to lock your Ford. Easy, too. Just insert your key, give a ¼ turn to the right and your car will be there when you return. Corbin lock, each one different. Not necessary to raise hood to lock. Easily put on."

A similar type of theft protection was in the mid twenties' ads for a product called Mixolock, which when added to the Ford carburetor, produced the usual astounding results. The copy relative to theft protection was near the end of the company's pitch, almost as an afterthought. The copy involved read, "To prime motor, remove cap and squirt gasoline direct into manifold. When this cap is removed no one can start engine as only fresh air is drawn into cylinders, which of course will not explode. It locks the car, and prevents theft."

Regarding personal safety in motor car operation, the autoist at the turn of the century was advised by Lady Dorothy Levitt: "If you are going to drive alone in highways and byways it might be advisable to carry a small revolver. I have an automatic Colt and find it very easy to handle as there is practically no recoil."

Chapter 13

Model T Powered Airplanes, Tractors, Trucks and Tanks

"Rescued from a grave in the junk heap,
Tin Lizzie dons working clothes and makes
money for the ingenious man who thinks of new
ways to use her cheap and ample power"

The Model T engine, sometimes removed from what was to be its final resting place—an old-car junkyard—was reactivated to power light aircraft to boats, not to mention myriad stationary applications.

Modern Mechanics and Inventions magazine was especially active in running articles on what to do with old Model Ts. In one of their late 1928 issues, for instance, they ran an article entitled, "New Uses for Old Fords," subtitled "Rescued from a grave in the junk heap, Tin Lizzie dons working clothes and makes money for the ingenious man who thinks of new ways to use her cheap and ample power."

The article began woefully: "Since the Ford Motor Company has ceased production on the universally known model T Ford car, millions of which are to be found in every corner of the world, many of these cars have drifted prematurely to vacant lots and garage junk heaps as an expectant public floods the Ford plant with a deluge of orders for the successor of the old design.

"Does this mean that Tin Lizzie has served the last days of her utilitarian life? On the contrary!

"New uses for the 'cast iron wonder' are being found daily wherever a need for extremely cheap and husky power comes up. In motorboats, converted tractors, power sleds, saw rigs, pump and well drilling outfits the familiar bulk of the gasoline heart of the old Tin Lizzie is seen more and more often these days. They are even being made into light aircraft engines!

"The Ford Model T motor can be bought for a price from $5 or $10 up to $25, depending on condition. No matter how worn, no matter how ready to 'kick the bucket,' the engine may be, repairs are to be had at the usual low prices in every garage. This will be the case for many years to come, for the parts replacement business of the Ford Motor Company is a huge industry in itself. So no matter what the condition

of the engine of old Model T, it can be bought with the assurance that it will provide serviceable power for years to come, and can be put in running condition at a low cost.

"One of the uses to which the Ford engine has been put with very satisfactory results is in the propulsion of boats. Developing 12 h.p. at 1000 r.p.m. the engine makes a very good power plant for driving runabouts, launches and small cruisers. Placed in an 18-foot runabout, a speed of about 18 miles an hour is easily obtainable, turning a 14-inch diameter by 16-inch pitch propeller wheel of three blades. A speed of eight to ten miles has been obtained in a fairly heavy open launch of 25 feet in length, using a 16-inch diameter by 16-inch pitch three-blade propeller. Boats as large as 35-footers have been driven 7 to 8 miles an hour by the Ford motor hooked to a 16-inch diameter by 14-inch pitch wheel.

"As it is a unit power plant, there is very little alteration needed to make a motorboat engine out of the Ford engine. One of the most effective ways of converting the mill from automobile use is to install the motor together with the frame on the usual wooden engine beds such as are built into the boat. The illustration shows this method plainly.

"A four-inch Lobee gear pump obtainable from any marine hardware house will fit the crank-saddle bolt to perfection, and a coupling for driving it can be made by drilling the timer housing and running the shaft through on a specially made small timer nut. This cares for the cooling water system.

"Fitted with steel wheels, with tractor lugs and an extremely low gear attachment, many an old Tin Elizabeth is now grinding out the last hours of her existence in some truck gardener's potato patch, doing light work like harrowing, drawing the cultivator, and hauling spray outfits. If the soil is not too heavy, these will even do a creditable job of pulling a single bottom with ease.

"As a tractor, aside from the changes mentioned, the only additional equipment needed is the belt driven type of pump, needed to circulate the water faster, thus cutting down on oil consumption."

In an early 1929 issue, *Modern Mechanics and Inventions* ran an article entitled, "Ford Powered Motor Boats." The illustration accompanying the article was captioned "The Ford auto engine, Model T, makes a splendid boat motor with the proper changes."

The article began, "Conservation of natural resources by reclaiming waste materials and converting them into useful and valuable products is one of the main problems occupying the attention of science today. Utilization of the waste represented in wornout and obsolete motor cars is such a problem. Annually thousands of automobiles are junked, despite the fact that a large percentage of them contain useful motors which might be converted to practical needs on farms or in industry where motor power is essential.

"Of one particular type of automobile motor alone, the Model T Ford, there have been more than 15,000,000 manufactured. At agencies or at wrecking yards, there are thousands of these motors which can be purchased for around $3.50 each and can be reconditioned at a cost of $5 to $25 apiece, making it possible to get years of service in driving boats, farm and shop machinery and other work where power is required. The conversion is simple but due to particular features of the Ford motor, the same parts, interchangeable with this type of motor, may not convert to any other make of motor.

"Attempts made by experimenters to date, not familiar with the peculiar construction of the Model T engine, to adapt the engine to new uses, have often resulted in failure. The principal reason has been because of burned out bearings, resulting from the thinning out of the oil and from inadequate water-cooling—not a problem when the engine has been used in automobiles. The original thermo-siphon method of engine cooling will not work on marine use."

In the early thirties, *Modern Mechanix* (using a revised title) published several homebuilt aircraft plans,

The varied uses to which an old Model T engine can be put.

including the Pietenpol Air Camper and the Gere biplane, using either Model T or Model A engines.

In 1932, *Popular Mechanics* magazine ran an article entitled, "Portable Power Plants from Old Auto Motor."

"With the body removed and the frame cut in two even with the rear part of the transmission, an old Model T Ford makes a good power plant that is easily moved and occupies little space when stored," the article began.

"Two legs of bar iron, bolted to the universal housing to support the rear end, are fitted with angle-iron feet and braced as indicated. The driveshaft housing is cut off as shown, welded to the transmission and then babbitted to take a 1⅛-in. shaft, one end of which is squared to fit into the transmission assembly.

"A 1⅛-in. iron washer is placed inside of the bell-shaped housing, and a hole drilled through the shaft, just in front of the washer for a large cotter key to hold the assembly in position. A belt pulley of suitable size

is mounted on the end of the projecting shaft. It is a good idea to make a catch fitting over the clutch pedal, to hold the transmission in neutral. A towing handle is made to fit over the rear end of the frame, while the wheels can be locked rigidly by bolting lengths of flat iron between the steering arms and the spring shackle bolts."

Modern Mechanics and Inventions ran in another 1929 issue an article entitled, "New Uses for Old Fords Contest," subtitled "*Modern Mechanics* will pay $10 for acceptable photos of every odd use to which old Model T Fords have been put. The queer machines shown below are made from old 'Tin Lizzies.'

"Up in Minnesota where the water is sky blue many sportsmen sojourn during the summer," the article began. "These same sportsmen use motorboats and demand clear, weedless lakes from their hotel and resort keepers. Further, so as to vex these resort opera-

The Ford auto engine, Model T, makes a splendid boat motor with the proper changes.

Another article from Modern Mechanics *magazine of late 1929 on how to convert a Model T engine for marine use.*

Build this Ford-Motored Boat!

Hᴇʀᴇ'ꜱ "Gannet," a neat twenty-foot cruiser, powered by a converted Model T Ford engine, which is a boat ideally adapted to the needs of the home builder who wants a creditable ship that can be constructed at a minimum of expense. It was designed especially for Modern Mechanics and Inventions by Charles H. Hall, noted naval architect, who bore in mind the needs and limitations of the amateur builder when drawing up the plans. "Gannet" is a sturdy boat that will bear up well under rough service. She'll develop ten to fifteen miles an hour. Build her from a set of large-size blueprints made from Mr. Hall's original drawings—Modern Mechanics and Inventions' Blueprint Department **$2.00** will send them to you postpaid for ....

TWO-PLACE AIRPLANE PLANS

Build the Pietenpol Air-Camper — a two-place parasol monoplane, powered with a Model A Ford motor. A remarkable performer which can be built for less than $500 complete. Blueprints on this ship, showing construction details and motor conversion, will be sent postpaid for $7.50.

"PUNKIN SEED," an Outboard Racer

"Punkin Seed" is a fast hydroplane which is extremely simple to build, and which develops a speed of around 40 miles an hour with a standard outboard motor. She's strictly a one-man boat—easily portable. Blueprints made from the designer's original drawings will be shipped postpaid for 75c.

Other Plans in Preparation. Address

Modern Mechanics and Inventions

BLUEPRINT DEPARTMENT

529 South Seventh Street   **Minneapolis, Minn.**

A 1931 announcement that plans for a 20 ft. cruiser powered by a Model T engine were available from Modern Mechanics *magazine, which had previously published the plans and engine conversion.*

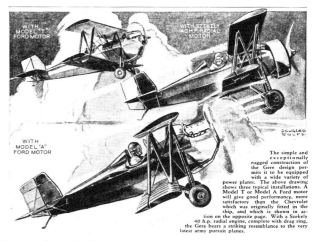

The simple and exceptionally rugged construction of the Gere design permits it to be equipped with a wide variety of power plants. The above drawing shows three typical installations. A Model T or Model A Ford motor will give good performance, more satisfactory than the Chevrolet which was originally fitted in the ship, and which is shown in action on the opposite page. With a Szekely 40 h.p. radial engine, complete with drag ring, the Gere bears a striking resemblance to the very latest army pursuit planes.

Plans for both the Pietenpol Air Camper and the Gere Biplane, published in Modern Mechanics *magazine, powered by either the Model T or Model A engine.*

151

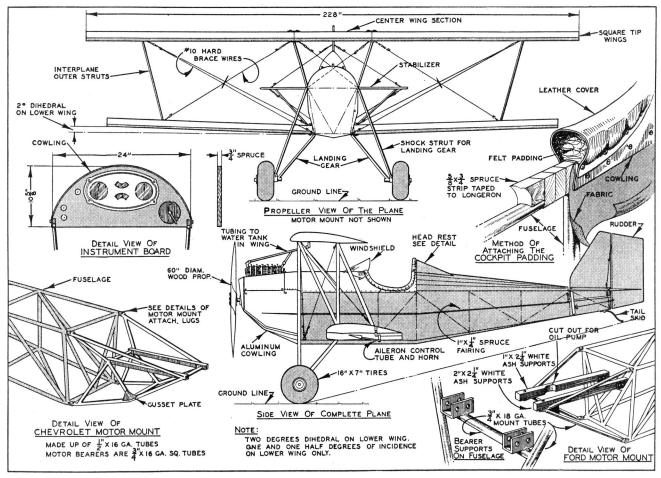

Gere Sport Biplane plans.

tors, weeds have a habit of growing very thickly in certain lakes. One hotel keeper solved the problem with a weed cutter made from an old Ford. The machine is

in daily use during the summertime near Melrose, Minn.

"The drawing gives a very clear idea of how pontoons are made from old oil barrels, fastened together

A portable power plant developed from a wrecked Model T, from a 1932 issue of Popular Mechanics magazine.

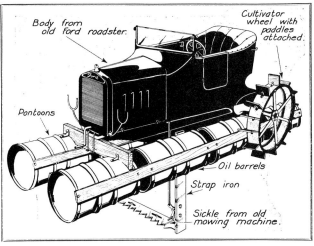

A hybrid device based on a Model T Roadster, used to cut lake weeds, the bane of serious fishermen in Minnesota.

with carriage bolts to a long substantial plank, and how the old Ford Roadster body is mounted on the 'chassis.'

"The steering arrangement is particularly novel. The wheels which drive the boat are paddle wheels made from the rolling members of an old cultivator to which oak paddles are fastened by means of a series of strap iron angles. When the pilot of this queer cornfield schooner wishes to swing his craft to port or starboard, he brakes the opposite wheel. This speeds up the other through the differential and the craft laboriously makes its change of course.

"Even an old Ford engine is plenty good enough for use as a rat exterminator. Maybe the motor has a bad piston slap, loose connecting rod, and badly worn bearings, but these little imperfections won't affect its efficiency a bit when it comes to poisoning prairie dogs, gophers, or other pests which annually cost the country millions of dollars through their depredations.

"Every automobile owner knows that carbon monoxide is one of the products of combustion in a gasoline engine, and he knows that it is a deadly gas. Carbon monoxide has taken the lives of many unwary motorists who ran their engines in an unventilated garage. An Ohio farmer, considering these facts, wondered why he couldn't use his old Ford to exterminate a large family of field rats which were making severe inroads into his crops.

"He secured a length of rubber tubing, threw a shovel into the back seat of his car, and drove out to his field. It was easy enough discovering the entrance to the animals' burrows, and a simple task to attach one end of the tubing to the exhaust pipe of his car. The other end he inserted in the tunnel leading to the animals' under ground home. A shovel full of earth packed the tube into the ground around the opening so

that it was air tight. Then he started his engine, let it run for a minute or two, and the deed was done."

Another issue of *Modern Mechanics and Inventions* showed another winner of $10 for his "ingenious old Ford air compressor."

Under the accompanying drawing, the article began with "Down at Iowa Park, Texas, is an old flivver motor which is enjoying a ripe-old age, puffing and grunting on half her lungs, while the other half supplies fresh ozone for tires which have lost the courage of their convictions.

"The two front cylinders have been manifolded off from the rest of the motor by the simple expedient of hack-sawing them off where they were not needed, and bunging the ends with welded plate iron.

"The intake valves of the rear pair of cylinders were loaded with springs to keep them depressed, and the exhaust valves were brazed in tightly. The spark plug hole was fitted with half-inch pipe and this in turn led to check valves after the air stream had passed by relief or globe valves installed to care for the extra pressure. Once past the check valves, the air was conduited by pipe to a storage tank.

"A special boiler full of water was provided for the thermo-siphon system, as doing this kind of work was impossible without some adequate means of cooling. If you don't think the motor works to pump air, you ought to see the water steam!

"This novel use for an old Ford keeps a garage supplied generously with compressed air."

Ford Model T tractor conversions

Conversion to a tractor was the old Model T's biggest and most important accomplishment, however. By comparison, the other efforts were mostly novelties

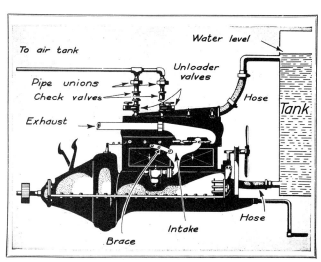

A Model T engine using two cylinders to compress air and two cylinders as motive power.

A Model T converted into a tractor with the addition of some professionally made wheels.

and of little importance. One might even say that the Ford Motor Company recognized the Model T as the basis for a tractor, consequently producing side-by-side with the T, the Fordson tractor. This didn't prevent dozens, if not hundreds, of homemade efforts to convert old Model Ts into useful farm vehicles.

The June 1916 issue of *Popular Mechanics*, for instance, ran an article entitled "Outfit Changes Motor Car to Tractor or Truck." The accompanying illustration from the article shows the professional-looking result obtained.

"By means of a special outfit, or set of parts, for which patent rights have been granted a Minneapolis inventor, any light motor car can be converted into a farm tractor and used for plowing, cultivating, harrowing, and similar purposes" began the article. The fact that the name Ford Model T was not mentioned as being the basis of the inventor's prototype is due to the magazine's policy of never mentioning commercial products by name. No free advertising in *Popular Mechanics*!

"The particularly interesting feature of the scheme," continued the article, "is that the equipment

Another Model T converted to a tractor, this one using the rear wheels of an old tractor.

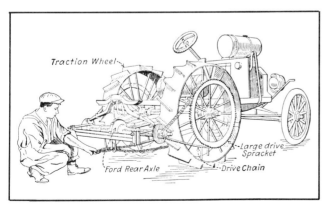

A Ford Runabout converted to a tractor using the Knickerbocker conversion unit.

may be applied or removed quickly so that the machine can be used for both utilitarian and pleasure purposes. Furthermore, if it is desired, truck wheels can be applied to the rear axle and the car used instead of a wagon or as a good tractor. The rubber-tired wheels are replaced with large metal ones and a chain-and-gear driving system employed.

"The power is supplied at two points opposite each other and several inches from the center of the bull wheel, so that, according to the inventor, it is not necessary to use roller bearings to take up the strain. A liberal road clearance is given and all gears encased in oil. It required but thirty minutes to change almost any car into a tractor capable of pulling two 13-inch plows.

"In another ten minutes, the truck wheels can be applied. The speed of the fan is increased and a circulation pump installed. The outfit includes a belt attachment which enables power to be transmitted to various farm implements, such as separators, balers, and corn shellers," the article concluded. The fact that the transformation required the installation of "a circulation pump" is a virtual dead giveaway that a Model T was used as the inventor's prototype.

A more direct application of tractor rear wheels to a still-kicking Model T can be seen in the accompanying photo from 1919. The attaching items were professionally made by the Knickerbocker Motors Company and sold under the brand name Forma-Tractor.

The following review of the product is taken from a 1919 trade journal: "At a time when the development of the country's agricultural resources is of greatest import, the announcement of an attachment that will turn anyone of the million odd Fords in the country into an efficient tractor for all kinds of cultivating purposes is particularly significant and of great importance to the farmer.

"This device is simple in construction, but sufficiently rugged to stand the strain of the work in the field and has the efficiency of a four-horse team for ploughing and cultivating and haulage purposes. It will not only permit the farmer to handle his cultivation problems with great economy and dispatch but is so adapted to his Ford that it can be attached or detached within less than thirty minutes, and therefore will not deprive him of the use of his car as a pleasure vehicle or for carrying produce to the market."

Under the heading of, "Tractor Attachments for Ford," Victor W. Page in his *Models T and A Ford Cars* writes, "The power and reliability of the Ford engine makes it possible to use this light chassis for much heavier work than one would imagine it capable of. A variety of tractor attachments are provided by which the Ford chassis may be used for light agricultural work such as plowing, harrowing, cultivating, etc. A practical attachment of this nature is shown in the accompanying drawing.

"The drive is by chain with a pinion sprocket fitted to the ends of the ordinary Ford axle and a large ring sprocket connected to the drive wheel. It is claimed that in the lighter type of tractors, it is a common failing that the front wheels are lifted from the ground due to the force of the drive and the drawbar pull. A study of the attachment shown will bring out the fact that in pulling the trailer, the front wheels are held on the ground by virtue of the fact that the drawbar attachment is forward of the rear wheels, which act as a pivot point upon the ground.

"The tractor is known as the Aca-Tractor chain-driven unit. This is a self-cleaning chain due to the fact that it operates around a very narrow angle on the sprocket. One of the advantages claimed for the unit is its short wheelbase. This is due to the fact that the drive-wheels are placed in front of the Ford axle and has the advantage of being able to make a short turn in plowing and other field operations.

"Probably the greatest difficulty which Ford tractor attachments have had to contend with is in the supply of cooling water. The method used in the Aca-Tractor to increase the radiator capacity is to mount above the engine a tank holding 11 gallons, making a total of 16 gallons of water in circulation. By setting the drive wheels close to the frame, the front and rear wheels track in the furrow. This tends to reduce the pull in plowing. To attach the machine to the Ford chassis requires about 3 hours.

"Another conversion set for tractor work is known as the Make-a-Tractor and, while shown fitted to a Ford chassis, it can be fitted to other passenger cars as well. The type A is used especially on the Ford, for which it was originally designed. The form at B is the adaptable type for other cars, although it too can be used on Fords. It is claimed by the manufacturer that this device can be attached in from 15 to 20 minutes, ready for work in the field. The various features include an auxiliary cooling system, consisting of a specially designed fan and a centrifugal pump, to aid in keeping the power unit cool when working under severe conditions. An attachment to the carburetor to prevent dust entering the engine is also supplied.

"In mounting the attachment, the rear wheels of the motor car are removed and the two driving pinions which mesh with the bull gear on the tractor wheels are attached. All implements are pulled by the attachment itself, thus relieving the chassis of the motor car as much as possible from the strain of the work. Traction is secured by the semi-concave creepers shown in the illustration. An attachment is also provided by which belt power can be had for various kinds of farm work. Special pinions are also provided for road work which

give a speed of about 6 m.p.h. The maker states that this attachment will do the work of 4 to 8 horses and will plow about one-third more acreage than horses."

Ford Model T tanks

While it may not be completely accurate to list Ford's World War I tank production under "Other Uses," they may just get in under the wire as the tanks produced were powered by Model T engines—two of them, actually, albeit new ones.

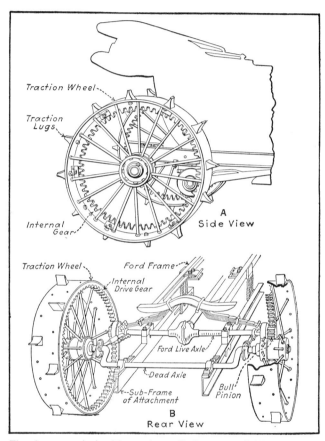

The Acason chain-drive unit applied to a Model T.

The Make-a-Tractor unit applied to a Model T.

On March 25, 1918, Henry Ford issued a statement calling for 90,000 two-man tanks, which he felt his factories were capable of producing—if the war lasted long enough. Ford assured the country that he could produce a tank that could "resist the hail of machine-gun bullets and shrapnel splinters." With its two-man crew, it "would have the offensive power of 50 soldiers with rifles."

Encouraged by such confidence, the Ordnance Department of the Army gave the Ford Motor Company the go-ahead to develop such a tank. Never one to do things by halves, the Ford Motor Company began developing plans for two distinct designs simultaneously. The smaller two-man tank was to be powered by two Model T engines, coupled to the regular epicyclic transmission. The larger design envisioned a three-man crew and was to be powered by two Fordson tractor engines.

After viewing the tests of the smaller prototype on October 1, 1918, near River Rouge, during which the two-man tank attained a top speed of 8 mph, the Ordnance Department issued a contract for 15,000 of the smaller tank. An order for 1,000 of the larger tank was subsequently received but by the time full-scale production could get under way on either of the tanks, the Armistice was signed.

Only fifteen small tanks appear to have been built. These were shipped to France after Armistice and used primarily to tow guns and Quartermaster stores trailers. None ever saw any action.

Ford Model T airplanes

Ford's interest in producing aircraft originated in 1924 with his association with William B. Stout. Their first venture was a single-engined corrugated aluminum-bodied aircraft, the forerunner of the later Ford

AIR FLIVVER READY TO FLY WEIGHS ONLY 1,000 POUNDS

Model of Henry Ford's new flivver of the air shows how the 1,000-pound plane will look as it is in flight. Its designer calls it the flying counterpart of the famous "Tin Lizzie."

At left, air flivver with wings removed showing how propeller is guarded. At right, William B. Stout, designer of the new plane.

Above right, a model of the Sky Car. Below left, the prototype Sky Car with wings removed, showing propeller guard. Bottom right, William B. Stout, plane designer, sitting in the prototype. Plans for actual production never actually developed due to the Depression. Mr. Stout is remembered more for his super-streamlined cars of the mid thirties, none of which ever reached production either.

tri-motor transports. The first scheduled airline flight with a tri-motor was made April 13, 1925, and first contract mail flight was made February 15, 1926, the same year the Stout Metal Aircraft Company, a division of the Ford Motor Company, was founded. Production of the tri-motor transports began in June 1926 and ended in 1933. It is reported that Ford lost some six million dollars on the venture, trying to popularize aviation.

Ford also made an effort to produce a flying flivver during the same period. *Popular Science* in its June 1931 issue ran the following story under the heading, "Air Flivver Ready to Fly Weighs Only 1,000 Pounds."

The copy began, "Reports have long had it that Henry Ford, the man who made cheap automobiles, was about to produce a light plane that any man could afford to own and fly. Now Ford's chief aircraft designer, William B. Stout, announces that he has what he calls 'an aerial counterpart of the famous Tin Lizzie.' This little two-seater plane was recently exhibited in Detroit. It was expected to be placed on the market soon, probably to sell for less than $2,000, and plans for quantity production have been made.

"Within one of these novel metal planes, the driver of one of the first flivvers would feel right at home. A brake lever at the pilot's left, suggesting the emergency brake of early Ford cars, locks the plane's wheels while the motor warms up. Foot pedals like those on the old cars control the plane's lateral rudder. Even the ignition switch and self-starter button are familiar to Ford drivers, but the dashboard has many dials not found in cars.

"The plane weighs less than 1,000 pounds, and is said to be able to land in the space of a tennis court if necessary. It has a forty-three-foot wing spread. The seventy-five-horsepower motor drives a pusher propeller, carefully shielded by framework so that no one can blunder against it while the plane is on the ground.

" 'For the present,' says the designer, 'the plane is called the Sky Car, though the public, in its usual fashion, is likely to dub it something much less formal.' "

Ford Model T Trucks
The precursor of the pickup truck was a custom- or homebuilt truck, often using the Ford Model T car as the foundation. A beautiful, rare example resides in the Denver, Colorado, Veteran Car Museum: a 1915

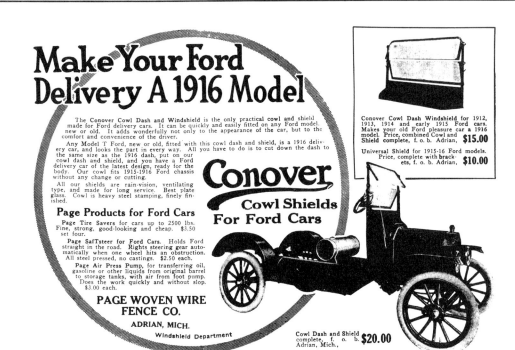

By adding the above cowl dash and windshield, an owner could bring his earlier model up to a 1916 model.

A 1915 Model T restored by Veteran Car Museum, Denver.

158

Model T "C" cab pickup truck. Ford did not build any of the wooden bodies on their early cars; wagon makers, cabinet makers and coachbuilders constructed the early bodies to the order of and need of the new owner. The Model T "C" cab pickup was built by the Emerson Brantingham Company Carriage Works of Rockford, Illinois. The body is made of oak with navy striping. The cab has navy blue metal side panels, long grain top and a black interior. The hood and fenders are also black.

In 1925, *Popular Mechanics* magazine ran two articles on Ford trucks worth reprinting. The first of these was entitled, "Swinging Booms on Service Car." Copy began: "By mounting two swinging booms made of heavy pipe and fittings, on the chassis of a light automobile made over into a service car, an Alabama dealer increased its usefulness considerably.

"The two booms are fastened together at the rear with two cross members of iron. Recently the car was sent out for a one-ton truck loaded with lumber, which had gone over a 20-foot embankment. The truck was pulled up without unloading it. This was done by swinging the two booms at right angles to the car, anchoring one to a tree on the side of the road opposite the wreck, while the other boom was used in pulling up the truck."

The other article was entitled, "Removing Ford-Truck Engines," and began, "Considerable difficulty usually attends the removal of the engine from a Ford

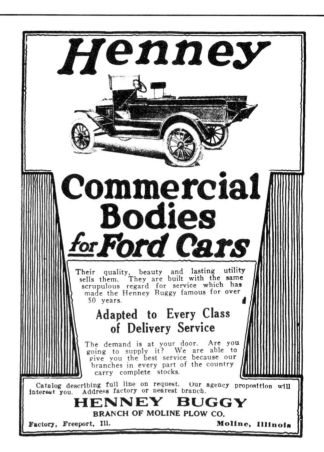

Ad, circa 1920, offering truck bodies for the Model T.

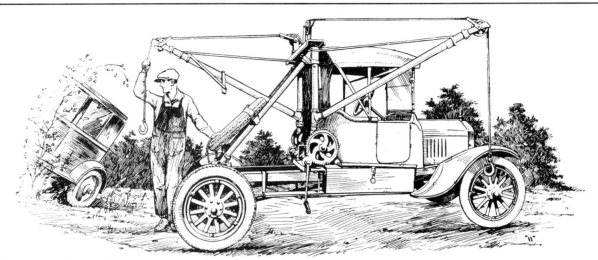

Ford tow-truck conversion.

truck, due to the interference of the dash and of the exhaust-pipe connection. In an eastern shop maintaining a number of these trucks, the trouble was overcome by sawing a slot in the dash from the inside to the steering post, as shown, so that the dash can be taken off without loosening the steering post. The exhaust and muffler pipe are pulled out as a unit by disconnecting the clamps that hold the manifold to the cylinder block. It is then an easy matter to remove and replace the engine."

Model T commercial conversion for the Railway Express Agency.

Model T United Parcel Service commercial conversion.